"With humor, grace, and real depth, Leon Neyfakh's book does the heady work of trying to understand what makes an artist, and whether one can live in the world as we have organized it."
—Lena Dunham, author of
Not That Kind of Girl

"I've never met Leon Neyfakh, and I wouldn't recognize Juiceboxxx if he knocked on my front door and literally offered me a box of juice. But this is a great book about the intractable dissonance between loving art, wanting art, and being an actual artist. The story is small, but the ideas are massive."
—Chuck Klosterman, author of *Fargo Rock City* and *Killing Yourself to Live*

"*The Next Next Level* is an intriguing look at the pursuit of an artistic lifestyle. Leon Neyfakh writes as a fan and friend about musician and performer Juiceboxxx, and in doing so he honestly uncovers the personal sacrifice and uncertainty that most artists wrestle with daily. It's a new and worthwhile look at some big questions surrounding creativity."
—Craig Finn,
The Hold Steady

"Are artists different from other people, or do they just not know any better? The myth of the Romantic genius is alive and well, to judge by Leon Neyfakh's fascination with the underground musician Juiceboxxx, and as Neyfakh struggles to understand the myth, and its extreme forms two centuries after Byron, he proves as thoughtful as Friedrich Schiller and as funny as Geoff Dyer." —Caleb Crain, author of *Necessary Errors*

"In *The Next Next Level*, Leon Neyfakh traces the career of underground musician Juiceboxxx, and teases out the internal conflicts that dog everyone, not just obscure rappers: adult vs. child, professional vs. enthusiast, artist vs. spectator, good vs. bad. Neyfakh is empathic and precise, leaving you unsure of which side you'd pick when—as Neyfakh and Juiceboxxx both do—you have to choose." —Sasha Frere-Jones

"In his journalism, Leon Neyfakh tends to tackle the murk and miracle of deep thinking, trends, history, and the law. With Juiceboxxx, he's dared to confront a more ambiguous idea: the murk of the self. Neyfakh wanted to write a profile. He found, instead, a moving, invaluable, acutely sensitive case study of what drives some of us to remain who we inexorably are." —Wesley Morris

"In his eloquent look at a fascinating musician, Leon Neyfakh explores the difference between an artist and a fan and suggests that for those Americans under thirty, there is no difference between high and low culture. An enthralling double portrait of the performer and the observer and a meditation on the passage from adolescent dreams to adult assessments." —Edmund White, author of *City Boy*

THE NEXT
NEXT LEVEL

THE NEXT NEXT LEVEL

A STORY OF RAP, FRIENDSHIP, AND ALMOST GIVING UP

LEON NEYFAKH

 MELVILLE HOUSE
BROOKLYN · LONDON

THE NEXT NEXT LEVEL

First Melville House Printing: July 2015

Everything in this book really happened. All quotes are
accurate, with the exception of a handful that were
reconstructed from memory. Several moments were
rearranged for clarity.

Grateful acknowledgment is made for permission to reprint
the following photographs: page 11, courtesy of Ike Sriskandarajah;
and page 13, courtesy of Lisa Locascio

Melville House Publishing   8 Blackstock Mews
46 John Street   and   Islington
Brooklyn, NY 11201   London N4 2BT

mhpbooks.com   facebook.com/mhpbooks   @melvillehouse

ISBN: 978-1-61219-446-2

Printed in the United States of America
10 9 8 7 6 5 4 3 2 1

A catalog record for this book is available from
the Library of Congress

For my mom, who liked this book even though it's about a rapper,
and for my dad, who I think would have liked it, too

"If you don't have good dreams, Bagel, you got nightmares."

—Boogie, *Diner*

CONTENTS

INTRODUCTION

When I saw him this past January, I asked Juiceboxxx directly if I was right to suspect that I had inadvertently ruined everything. I laughed as the words came out of my mouth, because the possibility that he would say, "Yeah, actually," or even, "Yeah, kind of," was too horrible for me to fathom with a straight face. Juice had been a free man before he decided to let me be his friend; he may have been living an uncertain, not very comfortable life, but at least he was in his own lane, his hands gripping the wheel even as he swerved, skidded, and stalled. Then I came along and made the myopic assumption that what was best for me, a journalist with a wife, a dog, and a savings account, was also best for him, a turbulent and ambitious artist with dreams I never had a chance at understanding. True, he had asked me to tell him if I heard about any job opportunities. Nevertheless, it was because of me that he ended up pursuing one, and in the process, became a participant in something almost unthinkably ordinary.

On paper it didn't sound so bad: I had given his name to two former colleagues of mine, who had e-mailed everyone in their professional network saying they had just taken over a fancy magazine about contemporary art, and were looking to bring in new people who could work a few days a week for not very much money. Juiceboxxx, at this time, was making ends meet by writing TV jingles and DJing parties, and living in the basement of a house in Far Rockaway where he paid two hundred dollars a month to sleep on the floor behind a bar. A weekly paycheck, it seemed, would be useful to him.Among other things, it would allow him to finally pay the guy he had hired to put the finishing touches on his new album.

I thought I was helping. What I didn't think about was the possibility that having an office job for the first time in his life, and spending his days writing articles and blog posts about other people's art, could throw Juice into a seriously dislocating existential crisis. I began to worry, after he was hired and started going in to work, that the simmering sense of panic that had always infused his entire being, not to mention his music, would thin out, evaporate, and float away.

Among other things, having this job meant doing work under his legal name instead of under "Juiceboxxx"—something he had never done before. It also meant that he soon had a room of his own in a decent Brooklyn apartment, and could predict with almost 100 percent reliability where he would be at any given time of day.

"Did I destroy you?" I asked as we sat down to dinner in Soho, both of us coming from our respective offices.

Juice smiled and looked down at his food. It took him a minute to answer.

This little book, as you'll see if you keep reading, is about the difference between being an artist and not being one, and the confusion many people feel as they try to figure out which one they are, or should be, or wish they were. It's also about two guys colliding with each other at a crucial moment, and despite having roughly nothing in common, using one another as mirrors both for better and for worse.

During our early meetings in New York about two years ago, I spent half the time contorting myself in order to impress Juiceboxxx, and the other half resolving to present myself to him without fear or self-loathing, as the person I really was. The story here is about the ungainly and confusing grind that inevitably comes with shifting between those two gears.

More than anything else, this is a book about people trying to figure out what it is inside of them that makes them special, and then devoting themselves to the hard work of making it legible to the outside world. It's both a portrait of my idol—a talented outsider who has spent his life, figuratively and somewhat literally, running away from home—and a memoir about defining yourself through your taste, only to discover that the things you love don't easily fit with who you think you are, or who you were supposed to be. Juiceboxxx leveled with me, sometimes deliberately and sometimes by accident, during the months I spent following him around and interviewing him. In the subsequent pages I will level with you, and with him.

THE NEXT
NEXT LEVEL

1

DO IT YOURSELF

1.

I wish I could say that it's been years since I've thought of Juiceboxxx when he tells me, out of the blue, in a text message one night in September, that he's coming to New York. The truth is I have been thinking about him a lot—periodically checking his blog, wondering what city he's living in, hoping he's doing all right. A series of videos he has started uploading to YouTube every week, in which he stares in a sickly manner into a camera and talks in awful circles about his upcoming projects, has left me with the distinct impression that he is on the verge of cracking up.

What he says in his text is that he wants to "link" with me when he gets into town. I'm surprised but touched that he's even thought to contact me. Even though we've known each other since we were in high school, I always figured he mostly saw me as nothing more than a fan he happened to cross paths with at an early age—someone he remembered and was aware of but never thought of as an actual friend. Occasionally he'd e-mail me to tell me he was playing a show somewhere in my vicinity, or that he had a new song he wanted me to hear, or a project he was raising money for. But I always assumed his life was full of people he had that kind of relationship with—minor characters he had met once or twice, who stayed invested in him long after he moved on.

This text message feels different. When I get it, I imagine him sitting somewhere far away, going through the contacts in his phone and sending up a flare to everybody he wants to see while he's in the city. The fact that I made his list comes as a pleasant, if confusing, surprise.

I wonder what he's doing in New York. Last I heard he was back home in Milwaukee after spending some time in Los Angeles, but my assumption has been that he's just been touring a lot, sleeping on couches and playing tiny basement shows all over the country, just as he has been the entire time I've been aware of him.

Aside from those guesses, my main insight into Juice's plans and state of mind has come from listening to the music he's been putting out, a lot of which has dealt explicitly with getting older, and becoming increasingly anxious about where his life is going. Juice has always been self-deprecating in his lyrics, but the newer material is decidedly different in tone from his early stuff, which was mostly lighthearted and funny fare about partying, having a good time, and in his words, "keeping it positive." Though he still has a sense of humor about himself, these days he raps a lot about how fucked he feels for having devoted his entire life to being a "cartoon character," and also about how resolved he is to keep running down the same road.

Juice's most recent release, a rambunctious and emotionally stormy mixtape that he put up online for free, sounded like the work of a person teetering on the edge of total disaster but nonetheless trying—desperately, only sometimes convincingly—to channel an inspirational message about the importance of doing what you love even when nothing is working out. The songs have mood swings, stumbling from proclamations about holding your head up high and never looking back into unflinchingly bleak stuff about being an irredeemable loser.

At twenty-seven years old, Juice has been in this mode for a while now, and while I could quote any number of his lyrics from the past few years to illustrate this, I can think of one in particular, from a song off his one proper album, *I Don't Wanna Go into the Darkness*, that sums it up nicely: "On the road, you're on the run / and you can't stop till you are done / but you're never done / and you'll never stop / this is not for fun / this is all you've got."

2.

I first met Juiceboxxx when I was in high school, through a guy named Willy Dintenfass who went to the same sleep-away camp as I did the summer after tenth grade. Willy lived in Milwaukee, played guitar in a grunge band, and wore a red knit hat everywhere he went. Despite being super-smart, he had decided not to go to college in order to pursue music instead. I thought he was the coolest person I'd ever met.

After camp ended, Willy and I talked a lot on AOL Instant Messenger, and one time he even took a bus to visit me in Oak Park, the town outside of Chicago where I grew up after my parents moved there from Moscow. Willy introduced me to music I'd never heard of, and he had an acidic way of joking around that I wanted badly to import into my own personality. During our chatting sessions he would regularly send me mp3s of his own music, which included solo stuff that he recorded at home on his computer, and songs he performed with his band. I listened to Willy's music as much as I listened to anything else in my collection; to this day I have a "Dintenfass" folder in my iTunes that contains hundreds of his demos, some of which I secretly burned onto a disc off his computer during a weekend when I stayed at his house.

A few months after we came home from camp, Willy wrote and recorded a song about me, with a chorus that went, "He's not just someone to pee on / he's my friend, he's Leon." I was very flattered and touched by this. (The lyrics referenced a story I'd told Willy about two jerks in my gym class who had spent an entire week secretly peeing on me in the swimming pool by standing close to me and pretending to be my friends.)

One day, after we'd known each other for maybe a

year, Willy asked me if I could think of any places in the Chicago-land area where his new band Doom Buggy could play an all-ages show. I had no idea but said I would look into it. I had seen rock bands made up of kids from my school perform in the basement of a local Unitarian church called Cornerstone, and figured I could ask a friend of mine, who played drums for a popular trio of tenth graders called Wrong Turn, to give me some pointers on how to book a concert there. I also figured I could ask him if Wrong Turn might want to be on the bill, so that some of my classmates might actually come. Happily, he obliged on both counts, and soon I had a date at Cornerstone Church on the books.

It was a few days before the show when Willy asked if it would be possible for a kid he knew named Juiceboxxx to play a short set as well. Juiceboxxx, Willy said, was a fifteen-year-old white rapper from the Milwaukee suburbs who had recently started performing at local rec centers and open mics. Willy sent me a few of his songs, including one called "The Declaration of Dopeness," which opened with a line rhyming "weenie" with "Fellini," and one called "Fast Food Anthem" about how much Juiceboxxx liked Pizza Hut and the Midwestern sub chain Jimmy John's. I remember listening to the songs on headphones in computer class and thinking Juiceboxxx was funny—sort of like a rapping Weird Al, except aggressively youthful.

At this point, in 2003, most white kids in our part of the country who were into music, including Willy and including me, were still starting rock bands. Some were beginning to make electronic music on their computers, but even that wasn't too common yet. Despite the fact that Eminem was at the height of his powers, deciding to be a white rapper was still an uncomfortable proposition.

Some of those who tried anyway dealt with the mismatch between who they were and what they were doing by being ultra-serious and cerebral. Others embraced the irony, and turned their insistence on rapping into a joke. That was the impulse behind consciously ironic hip-hop acts like MC Paul Barman—"I'm iller than the Iliad"—and MC Chris, who wrote songs about Star Wars and video games. The tongue-in-cheek approach these guys took to rap was known as "nerdcore," and because Juiceboxxx had big glasses, looked like a skinny dweeb, insisted on writing jokey lyrics, and had named himself Juiceboxxx, that's what he seemed to be at first: an ascendant nerdcore rapper from Wisconsin, i.e., the least respectable-sounding thing a musician could be.

Juiceboxxx's songs were goofy and kind of embarrassing in parts—"I can rock the mic in any season / I'mma flip up my flow just for no reason"—but I liked them so much when I heard them that I was immediately seized with a desire to play them for everyone I knew. And so I told Willy I would be very happy if Juiceboxxx played a set, as long as it was OK if he went first. With that, I made new posters, some with a photo of Juice in which he looked extra pale and extra nerdy that said, "Come see this man rap," and some with his bespectacled face super-imposed onto the cover of *Get Rich or Die Tryin'* by 50 Cent.

On the night of the show, I did my best to stay calm even as the van carrying Juice, Willy, and Willy's bandmates was held up in traffic with minutes to go before Juice was due on stage. As the sun set, I waited for them outside, pacing up and down the street and tersely saying hi to friends as they approached the venue.

Seconds after the van finally pulled up, a tall, gangly, and distracted-looking guy bounded out of the backseat and asked me where the bathroom was so he could change into his jumpsuit. Before I knew it, Juiceboxxx was introducing himself to the crowd—no more than twenty people total had come—and asking no one in particular to turn his fucking amp up. Our chaperone for the evening, a man in his sixties named Dan who volunteered at the church and had been called upon to babysit us at the last minute, didn't know quite what to make of it all as he and I watched Juice from the back of the room. As the beat kicked in and Juice bounced on his heels in anticipation of his cue, he looked like a swimmer or a track star, poised on the starting blocks before the gun has gone off.

"You sure this guy is cool?" Dan said, glancing tentatively at me without taking his attention away from the stage.

"Yeah," I said, conscious of the fact that, even if I'd been confident in my answer, which I wasn't, nothing I could say was going to convince Dan not to worry. "OK," he said. "As long as you're sure all this won't get too crazy."

Together we watched as Juiceboxxx lunged from one side of the stage to the other, tearing at his hair, throwing himself to the floor, and leaping at the wooden beams that ran along the ceiling. He moved around with abandon, yelling into the mic with a hostility that brought to mind a singer in a punk band more than anything else. And yet, despite his jagged bounding around, Juiceboxxx used his hands like a professional rapper, stretching his fingers out and cutting the air with them.

Even as he delivered nerdcore-ish lines at his own expense—"This mic I destroy / I'm not a real rapper, yo, I'm just a decoy"—Juice held himself in a way that left us no choice but to take him seriously. And if he was making fun of himself, the joke was manifestly wrapped up in a thick layer of earnestness. Meanwhile, the hammy punch lines that I had originally latched onto when I heard Juice's mp3s faded deep into the background as he shouted unintelligibly and convulsed, sometimes staring at the floor and other times turning his head up at the audience with a snarl across his face.

He didn't seem angry, just possessed. With the jumpsuit and glasses that kept almost flying off his face, he looked like a total maniac, and when his top buttons came undone and he was left shirtless, there was something almost obscene about him, with his pink little nipples and his sharp elbows swinging wildly as he rapped. Though he didn't have much in the way of muscle, there was something in his physical presence that made him look as though he had been built specifically for what he was doing.

After reassuring Dan the chaperone, however tentatively, that there would not be any problems, I went looking for Willy and found him standing in the front row, dancing alongside the other members of his band. As Juice raged, his four friends from Milwaukee bobbed up and down with their stomachs out, their legs spread far apart, and their hands perched along their waistlines, where they kept time with the beat. Somehow these movements allowed them to project a detached, take-it-or-leave-it attitude while still being captivating. The perfect dance, I thought to myself.

Just then Juiceboxxx got out of a crouch, barreled into the crowd, and slammed violently into a horrified girl who had clearly come to Cornerstone to see Wrong Turn. After making sure she was OK I leaned in and said into Willy's ear, "Hey, do I need to be concerned?" to which he responded by smiling and shaking his head. "Don't sweat it," he said. "This is pretty much what always happens at a Juiceboxxx show."

I nodded, but noticed he specifically didn't say that everything would definitely be fine, or that Juiceboxxx would definitely not hurt anyone or break anything. Still, I let Willy's smile calm me down and tried half-heartedly to mimic his dancing style, as I would many times over the coming years. At one point Juiceboxxx bolted over to where we were standing, grabbed me by the ears with his clammy hands, and rapped at me with the microphone dangling from the crook in his elbow. It was the first good look I'd gotten at his face, which was dotted with zits and topped with a terrible haircut. He seemed to be in some kind of fugue state, and as I stood there with my eyes locked on his, I wondered if he knew that I was the one who had organized the show, or if I was just a random person to him.

After finishing his verse, Juice abruptly let go of me and, in a moment of apparent inspiration, launched himself at the ceiling with enough power to actually grab hold of one of the reinforcement beams. Once he had a grip on it, he began swinging like a monkey in a tree, his feet dangling several feet from the floor. This, understandably, was a bridge too far for Dan, who ran over to me and said into my ear, with some urgency, "Buddy, you've got to tell your friend not to do that." I didn't argue with him. But just as I was preparing to yank on Juice's pants, he got down on his own initiative, collapsing into a pile as the backing track faded into silence. After a few seconds of him lying motionless on the floor, it became clear the set was over. It had lasted maybe fifteen minutes.

People erupted into whooping and shouting as Juiceboxxx got up, disconnected the Discman that he had been using to play his beats, and made quickly for the exit. After a few minutes outside doing who knows what, he came back in and sold a bunch of copies of his EP, *2K3: The Year of the Juice*, and my friend Lisa, who I was in love with at the time, asked to take a picture with him.

Later, Juice stood at the front of the room, dancing and clapping his hands while Doom Buggy ripped through their set. Out of enduring loyalty to Willy I want to say that they rocked the house, but the truth is I don't remember anything about that night except Juiceboxxx.

3.

As it turned out, agreeing to add Juice to the bill was a pretty important decision for me and a bunch of my close friends, all of whom still remember the experience of watching him perform, and some of whom still have his early recordings stored on their hard drives. Seeing him that night exposed us to a species of teenager none of us had ever seen before, and in the years that followed his set, he took on the status of a mythical creature for us—a great, foreign force who had come out of nowhere, blown all our minds, and, with his first words into the mic—"What the fuck is up, Joke Park? My name is Juiceboxxx!"—left us with a nickname for our hometown that we still use to this day.

For years afterwards I watched Juiceboxxx from afar, aware that the life he lived was profoundly different from mine and that of practically everyone I'd ever been friends with. We were tame compared to him—good students who got into top-tier colleges and moved away from home to start our careers. Juiceboxxx, on the other hand, became a rootless wanderer: a guy who dropped out of the University of Wisconsin after one year and put himself in motion, subletting rooms for a week or a month at a time, paying his friends to sleep on their floors, and going on tour as much as he possibly could.

In the roughly twelve years that have passed since that night in the church basement, Juice has criss-crossed the continent and even toured Europe and Asia. And while he never really became part of any hip-hop scene, he did attach himself to a community of artists and musicians who operated at the margins of culture and self-identified as practitioners of a punk-based, DIY-inspired way of life. Juice's music, meanwhile, evolved at a rapid clip, absorbing disparate influences while growing progressively more different from anything most people I knew liked to listen to. For several years he took a detour into something one could accurately call dance-rap, and released four singles inspired by obscure genres of regional DJ music from Baltimore and Chicago. The biggest and best of these songs was "Sweat," which was built around a jangly, cheerful synth line and featured Juice chanting dance steps in a guileless tone that brought to mind "Pump Up the Jam" by Technotronic. Much to Juice's surprise, "Sweat" turned into a minor hit in the UK, getting him played on BBC Radio 1 and booked at all kinds of glitzy clubs full of glamorous Europeans—a far cry from the dingy venues he was accustomed to playing in the United States.

The dance phase lasted maybe two years, and ended with a song called "100MPH," whose chorus consisted of Juice simply repeating, over and over again, the phrase "One hundred miles per hour / One billion miles away." I remember writing it off at the time as depressingly lazy, but in retro-spect, it was the beginning of Juice's real flourishing as an artist: the moment when he started writing about himself and what it felt like to be Juiceboxxx.

The fact that Juice had made that leap came into focus for me in 2010, when he put out a mixtape called *Thunder Zone Volume 1*. The tape, which showcased Juice's now genuinely impressive skills as a rapper, opened with a one-minute intro built on top of the horn-heavy, up-tempo Bruce Springsteen song "Tenth Avenue Freeze-Out." While the song plays at a high volume, Juice, sounding deeply angry, determined, but also kind of joyful, delivers the following monologue:

> I know it's been a long time, man! I know I've been do-ing this shit for a long goddamn time! But if you think, for one *motherfucking second*, that I'm gonna give up now? After all the fuckin' shit I've been through, man? Well, let me tell you, mister: you've got another moth-erfucking thing coming.

Though I can't claim to have reacted very strongly when I first listened to it, I've come to see this as one of the most invigorating opening tracks I've ever heard—an electrifying declaration of purpose that manages to sound both vulner-able and bulletproof.

There were people who really responded to what Juice-boxxx was doing during this time, including a number of prominent figures, like the artist Cory Arcangel, the

producer Diplo, and Todd P, the influential New York pro-
moter known for throwing low-budget, independent concerts all over the city. And while it was hard for me to tell,
from the outside, how well Juice was doing, there were un-
ambiguous moments of triumph: collaborations with fash-
ionable DJs, guest verses from name-brand rappers, shows
with popular acts like Girl Talk and Dan Deacon. The high
point of this period was a tour in Canada opening for Public Enemy, during which Chuck D dubbed him "the Buddy
Holly of hip-hop." "SOMETIMES," Juice wrote on his blog
afterwards, "WHEN YOU KEEP ON RUNNING AND
DREAMING GREAT THINGS HAPPEN."

There were indications that more success was coming
to him. His album, *I Don't Wanna Go into the Darkness*,
though passed on by most of the record executives he sent
it to, was released on tape and on vinyl by a pair of small
but respected indie labels, and got positive attention from
cool media properties like *Vice*, *Impose*, and the website of
the street-wear company Mishka NYC. And yet, despite
all that—despite the fact that he has played shows in eighteen different countries, made YouTube videos that have
received tens of thousands of views, and has people roughly
my age all over the United States who can remember seeing
him play live—it is nevertheless true that Juiceboxxx is not
a famous artist, and that his music never gets written about
by *Pitchfork* or any of the popular hip-hop sites. Instead, his
success has taken on a form that is hard to pin down: oper-
ating on the fringes, he has won the support and respect of

some truly influential people in culture, but at the end of the day he has remained a secret to most.

It was after the Public Enemy tour, at the end of 2010, that Juice underwent his most recent evolution, which was inspired by an obsession with Springsteen that moved him to replace his Discman/mp3 player with a live band— including Willy on electric guitar—and start making what he openly, without embarrassment, described as rap rock. Depending on how you looked at it, taking this turn—and taking it a decade after horrible rap rock bands like Limp Biz- kit and Papa Roach turned that genre into a morbid punch line—was either an act of bravery or creative masochism.

4.

All told, I had seen Juiceboxxx perform maybe ten shows by the time I moved to New York after college—the last was in Chicago in June 2007, the month after I graduated. And though I usually made a point of coming up to him afterwards and saying hi, he has remained a largely abstract presence in my mind: a blurry character I have felt lucky to be aware of, despite not really understanding why I feel so drawn to him.

Over the years I've tried repeatedly to get people in my orbit interested in Juiceboxxx, and every time I've been disappointed by their reaction. Sometimes this has happened in the context of trying to talk someone into going with me to see him play live. Other times it's been while riding in someone's car and trying obnoxiously to steal their auxiliary cable in order to force them to listen to Juiceboxxx off my iPod. The sad fact of the matter is, while the friends of mine who watched Juice play in that church basement in 2003 still feel affection and even reverence for him, I don't think I've recruited more than one or two new people into the Juiceboxxx fan club over the course of my entire career as a Juiceboxxx evangelist. Most of the time, when I play Juice's music for people, they just don't like it. When I play it for Alice, my wife, she asks me to turn it off after thirty seconds.

And I get it. A lot of Juice's output is unequivocally off-putting, especially if you have no context for it. He shouts a lot, his voice is nasally, and some of the things he says are impossible to react to without looking down at your feet. As defensive as I get when Juice's talent is questioned or someone just doesn't get his appeal, I can understand why, unless someone's already on the rocket ship, they'd just want to get out of the way of his flailing.

You can see this happening sometimes at his shows, especially when he's opening for someone, which he usually is: Unless the crowd is full of loyal fans and friends who have loved him for years, he's likely to send at least a small contingent of confused people to the back of the room for drinks. In one clip I found online, he's nineteen and sitting on the ground shirtless and exhausted after finishing a set outside a venue somewhere in Canada, legs crossed and head hanging sullenly at his chest. "This is why you should have stayed in Wisconsin," some girl says to him, sneeringly, from outside the frame.

In the comments section of a 2010 article about Juice in *The A.V. Club*, some guy who had apparently gone to one of his concerts was more direct: "Juiceboxxx is awful. I have seen him live, and the gap ('yawning chasm' might better describe it) between his enthusiasm for the music and the crowd's made for one of the few truly uncomfortable concert experiences I've had. He was at the door as people were filing out, and we just had to avert our eyes."

I remember when I read that, I wanted to fucking kill that guy.

5.

When Juice texts me, a week or so after first making contact, to say he has arrived in New York, I write back, "Music to my ears!" and then ask him, "Where you staying?" It embarrasses me that I feel compelled to leave out the "are" in that sentence in order to sound casual, but I do. It is the first of what will be many moments when I strategically edit my personality in front of Juiceboxxx so as to convince him I am a guy it makes sense for him to hang out with.

Juice says he is staying in East Williamsburg, to which I respond, "Cool!" and tell him I'll have to spend a week in Boston for my job at some point during the upcoming month, but that otherwise I'll be around and up for hanging out. Juice responds, "Ya, lets link"—that word again—"it's truly been forever."

A few days later he invites me to go with him to see a band called Wavves at Irving Plaza. He is friends with the drummer, he says, and has a backstage pass with my name on it if I want to come. After thinking it over for a second, weighing the possibility that this will turn out to be my only shot at spending time with Juice, I turn the offer down because Alice and I are in the process of moving into a new apartment, and also because I have pretty conflicted feelings about Wavves, which I'll get into later, that make me really not want to see them, especially with Juice.

Luckily, another opportunity to link presents itself less than twenty-four hours later, while I'm at my friend Max Geller's apartment on the first Saturday night in October.

Max and I are on his couch talking when it occurs to me that maybe Juiceboxxx would want to come over and join us. The plan for the evening is to go sit around with Max's little brother Sam, an incredibly handsome twenty-five-year-old who plays guitar in a band that recently got one of their songs onto the *Girls* soundtrack. I picture him and Juiceboxxx talking shop, and wonder whether they would find any common ground.

Before I text Juice with an invitation, I decide I should make sure it's OK with Max, which makes me realize that, because Max and I are relatively new friends, he is one of the few people I am close to, besides my family, whom I have never talked to about Juiceboxxx.

"Does he have a name other than Juiceboxxx or is that what you call him?" Max asks—a reasonable question made harder to answer by the fact that, with the exception of one summer weekend after my freshman year of college (more on that later), Juiceboxxx and I have never spent any actual time together, which means I've never really called him anything.

After that first night we met, at the church, Willy reluctantly told me Juice's real name with the caveat that no one ever used it except his parents. Willy, along with all his other friends, always just called him Juice. This took me years to get used to, and even now, I feel nauseatingly unnatural saying it when I refer to him as "Juice" to his face. Maybe it's because I don't think of myself as someone who knows people with nicknames. Or maybe it's because "Juice" lands with a level of implied intimacy that I don't think is quite appropriate, given that I hardly know him. Whatever the reason, every time I say "Juice" I feel like I'm trying too hard to be something I'm not. And yet, the idea of addressing him as Juiceboxxx has always seemed even unwieldy—both because it's ridiculous, for its own reasons, and because it feels strangely like referring to someone by their first and last name.

I try to think, for Max's benefit, of the most succinct possible way to describe who Juiceboxxx is and why I care about him. Having gone through this a number of times in my life, I decide to take a shortcut, and propose showing Max a few minutes of a video someone made about him a few years ago—a sort of mini-documentary in which Juiceboxxx goes on tour and talks about why he has devoted his life to being a rapper. I feel a little self-conscious for suggesting it, as I always do when I make someone watch a YouTube video, and I'm relieved when Max agrees to sit through it.

The eleven-minute video, which follows Juice as he travels from Philadelphia to New York, was posted online in early 2012, right around the time *I Don't Wanna Go into the Darkness* was coming out. Though I've always been jealous of the person who made it—here was someone who had repped for Juiceboxxx more persuasively than I ever could—I've watched it so many times that I know it practically by heart: from the opening shot of Juice in a mustard yellow track jacket, sitting in a sun-drenched bedroom and telling the interviewer in a quiet, halting patter about his pseudonym;

to the scene on the Greyhound bus where he takes out a portable radio and talks about how he likes catching local stations on it when he's on the road; to the closing montage of him on stage, giving an airtight performance of a song called "Thunder Jam #5"—sample lyrics: "you roll down the window / and get on the road / everything feels so old / you feel like your head is gonna fuckin' explode"—in a pitch-black Williamsburg basement.

"That's what's so fucked up about where I'm at," Juice tells the interviewer at one point, speaking slowly, like he's terrified of putting his predicament into words. "It's just like, you know, when you fucking kind of have this identity based on this totally absurd premise—like, where do you go if you want to stop doing it, man? Like, where do you go?"

I'm psyched to see that Max, whose attention is not generally easy to keep, is captivated by the video—so much so that he watches to the very end, even though I offer to turn it off about halfway through after figuring that he's probably got the idea. "He seems like a pretty weird guy," Max says afterwards. "But yeah, let's get him over here."

6.

Juice arrives a little after midnight, and because in my mind Juiceboxxx is constantly barging into places, he surprises me by considerately calling my cell instead of ringing the doorbell.

We don't hug hello or anything, but I'm instantly excited about being in the same room with him and hearing his real voice come out of his real mouth after years of only hearing it in my headphones. We ask each other how it's going as I close the door behind him, and he says he's been trying to figure out how long it's been since we last saw each other. I've been thinking about the same thing, and the best I can come up with is that it's been more than seven years, since I know for a fact I haven't gone to a Juiceboxxx show since college. When I say this out loud it occurs to me that unlike everyone I know, Juice doesn't divide his life into pre- and post-college—that instead, he has all kinds of other, more singular reference points, like pre- and post-releasing an album, and pre- and post-opening for Public Enemy in Canada.

He has on jeans and a hoodie over a T-shirt that says "HIGH ROLLER" along the top and is decorated with a pair of dice and marijuana leaves. This makes me smile: though YouTube commenters are always speculating about Juice's substance abuse based on his antics and the dark circles under his eyes, I know from Willy that he has never been much of a drugs guy, and I suspect he likes the shirt only because "High Roller" was the name of an early Juiceboxxx song.

He's wearing a baseball cap on his head and white high tops caked with dirt on his feet. He looks a lot better than he did in his recent video diaries. As I watch him nervously push his glasses up the bridge of his nose with a single out-stretched index finger, I remember, in a flash, deciding years ago to start doing the same thing after seeing him do it during a performance.

We walk through the apartment and out into the back-yard, where I've been sitting with Max, his brother Sam, and a guy who has recently been brought on to play bass in Sam's band. I feel anxious about being a little drunk and I don't know exactly how to carry myself, because I'm trying to be someone Juiceboxxx would think is cool, while also acting normal in front of Max. "Guys, this is Juiceboxxx," I say, and as I hear the words come out of my mouth in a sing-song cadence, I think I sound like a parent introducing a room full of kids at a birthday party to a clown.

After everyone says hello and hands are shaken, Juice sits down in a lawn chair next to me and I offer him a beer, which he refuses. Though I really don't want to seem like I'm resorting to small talk right away, I ask him what he's up to in New York, which he answers with one word that underscores to me just how different his life is from mine: "Subletting." When I clarify that I meant, like, what he's doing, not what his living arrangements are, he says he's getting ready to put out on a new EP, and then go on a sixteen-date tour in November with Willy on guitar and an-other friend of his on drums. He has a month in New York before he ships out, he says. In the meantime, he's going to try to figure out if he can find himself some kind of job and move to the city on a permanent basis, so he can have a real home base for the first time in his adult life, and maybe his own room, after never having one anywhere except in his parents' house.

In an attempt to involve the others in our conversation, I ask Sam, who is smoking a cigarette across the table from me, whether his band has ever gone on tour. "Nah," he answers, looking and sounding a little sleepy at the thought of it. Hearing this, Juice gets interested, as I hoped he would, and follows up: "Oh, you play music?"

Sam explains his situation—that he plays guitar in one band that's been doing pretty well, but that his main focus is on a solo project that he's been writing songs for in anticipation of a gig in Brooklyn coming up next month. When Juice asks him why he doesn't want to tour, Sam says he doesn't really see the point right now, since there wouldn't be anyone in most cities who would go see him play. He'd rather just record music and put it online, he says, until someone notices it and writes about it. That way if he does go on tour, he reasons, people would actually show up.

I can see Juice isn't really into this answer, but he responds more diplomatically than I would have expected him to be capable of, telling Sam that, basically, yeah, that's the smart way to do it, but that he has a different outlook on it as someone who decided years ago to just tour incessantly and make that the backbone of his career. The problem is, Juice says, all the years he has spent on the road are a liability for him now, because thanks to the internet, an act with a long past turns out to be a lot less likely to break out than a young and fresh one. He explains that for the most part, people who write about music online are invested in discovering stuff no one else has heard of so that they can claim it as their own. That means that if you have twelve years of history like Juiceboxxx does, chances are no one's going to bother saying you're any good because there's nothing really in it for them to do so.

Sam backs him up on this, saying that friends of his who are in bands that have been picked up by labels or managers have been instructed to take down all their old music from the internet before they put out any new material. That way when they make their official debut, bloggers can feel like they're breaking them to the world by linking to them. One guy who recently came in for a lot of attention, Sam says, was apparently changing his name for years every time he put something out, so that each time it looked brand new and thus irresistibly alluring to the junior league tastemakers in a position to champion it.

Juiceboxxx says he's been told a million times that he should change his name—that friends in the music business have been trying to convince him to do so for years, but that, "for whatever stupid fucking reason," he keeps not doing it. This prompts Max to ask Juice if he knows of a young country musician I've never heard of who used to be called Jonny Corndawg. "Oh, sure, of course," Juiceboxxx replies. "I know Corndawg really well."

It turns out that "Corndawg," like Juice, spent a good

chunk of his twenties as a proud and devoted road warrior, playing tiny shows all over America and establishing himself within underground circles but never getting truly famous. Then one day he made a big move, as Juice explains it, by adopting the more sober-sounding moniker "Jonny Fritz," and soon after, he got signed to a huge indie record label co-founded by Dave Matthews from the Dave Matthews Band. Though he no longer has his name, Jonny is now an adult who makes good money playing music for a living.

"I don't know, man," Juice says, after recounting this story. Then, following a tense pause, he reiterates that Sam is making the right call playing it his way. He wouldn't recommend his career path to anyone, he says, if it weren't for the fact that he feels some stability knowing that he could never flame out the way a fly-by-night operation might. "In the twelve years I've been doing this I've stayed at a certain level," he says, sounding like a person trying not to come off arrogant but not really succeeding. "But if you're some buzz band it's easy to have a two-year rise and fall, because you don't have that circuit to fall back on."

As he says this I kind of brace myself, because I am worried Sam will feel like he's being lectured or insulted. But before I can interject, Juice continues, sounding increasingly defensive as he goes: "Like, I will always be able to go to any city in America and play to fucking thirty kids. And I mean, for most people that'd be fucking awful. And it kind of is. It's kind of the bleakest shit ever, in some ways. It is dark. Especially when you're twenty-seven, and you're like, 'Fuck, what am I doing with my goddamn life?' But at the same time there's something reassuring about it, because some buzz band won't even be able to do that."

He stops and no one says anything until Juice himself interrupts the silence. "Look," he says. "I am not advocating my dumb-ass lifestyle here, let me be fucking clear, all right? I think it's much better to be in a successful band for a couple of years and then, like, quit doing music and get a real fucking job."

He looks proudly fatalistic as he makes this declaration, but I'm convinced that deep down he doesn't really believe what he's saying. I wonder, in light of this, what he must think when he looks at me, a guy who's never had anything but a "real fucking job" in his life, and at this point, having achieved relative prosperity and a generally comfortable existence, very obviously never will.

Later, after pointing Juice in the direction of the nearest subway stop and flagging down a cab, I think about whether I'm going to see him again while he's in town, or if the evening that just ended will turn out to be it for us. Looking out the window as I'm being driven to my apartment, I imagine Juice waiting for the G train and getting home in an hour, and I become convinced there's no way he'd have any interest in hanging out with me a second time.

As I pay the driver and walk to my front door, I wonder what it was inside of Juiceboxxx that made him so different from me—why he went his way and I went mine, despite the fact that I had wanted so badly to be a little more like him and a little less like myself from the moment we met.

In the morning I have an idea, and after turning it over in my head for ten minutes in the shower, I send Juice a text message saying I want to interview him, so that I can write something about his life, his career, and the time he is spending in New York while pondering his future. "Sounds cool," he replies, and just like that, we make plans to get together two nights later.

2

AFFILIATIONS

1.

I wake up on the morning of my scheduled meeting with Juiceboxxx worrying that by interviewing him, I'll inadvertently upset him, or cause him to have destabilizing thoughts that he might not otherwise have. It occurs to me that by asking him certain basic questions—about what he's hoping to achieve in life, about what gives him the motivation to still perform as Juiceboxxx after all these years—I might send him into what he refers to in a lot of his recent songs as "the darkness," a state of mind in which all he can see is certain doom, the treacherously precarious nature of his situation, and worst of all, his own ridiculousness. ("I see the same faces every day / and I don't know why, but it doesn't make me feel OK / and every single time that the darkness comes around / it reminds me / that I gotta get out of town.") It seems potentially destructive, putting him through such a trial, especially at a moment when he seems to be taking a step forward in life by coming to a new city and trying to put down roots.

What I'm really afraid of, I realize after turning this over in my head, is playing some role in Juiceboxxx finally deciding to quit. I know as soon as I have this thought that it's probably based on an inflated sense my own potential influence. But it does seem like a real possibility that after spending a month opening up to someone like me about what it's like to suddenly find himself at twenty-seven lacking any stability or plans for the future, it would make sense in Juice's head to just hang it up, with our interviews serving as a sort of ceremonial closing of the book.

I feel lucky for having Willy on hand to ask about this. Willy, who still lives in Milwaukee and works in a sculpture garden, knows Juice better than just about anyone, and if anyone's in a position to tell me I should think twice about my little idea, it's him. He and Juice have been friends forever, and have gone on tour together countless times—not just in the early days, when Doom Buggy was still a going concern, but also later, when Willy started writing guitar parts for Juiceboxxx's songs and became a member of his backing band. Over the years I have occasionally asked Willy over Gchat about how Juice was doing, and he has filled me in on what his latest obsessions were, what his mental state was, how he was feeling about his station in life. On the one hand he talked about Juice as if he was unknowable, a force no one could tame or predict, but on the other he did so with an affection that made me think he understood him.

I write Willy an e-mail explaining briefly what I have in mind—that I want to follow Juice around during his time in New York, and interview him as he considers his next move and thinks about whether or not to settle in the city for good. I ask Willy if there's any reason he can think of that I should not do this.

He writes back:

> Def could be good. For 9–12 months now (maybe longer) he and I have had conversations in a pattern where he says he's hit a wall doing Juiceboxxx & he wants to do something else, but then there's always two or three more things he decides he has to accomplish. And usually in the interim, some small thing will break his way, and that will fuel him for a while. But then he'll get bummed about it again.

As for me wreaking any kind of havoc on Juice's psyche by making him talk about all his failures and frustrations, Willy encourages me not to worry. As far as he can tell, he writes, Juice tends to think about all that stuff a lot anyway.

Then there's a postscript that sends my eyebrows into my forehead:

> It's interesting that he's pitched it to you as
> deciding whether to live in NY. Does he
> mean that as in ending the project and doing
> some other job? 'Cuz I feel like that's the real
> thing he's considering.

This had not occurred to me. Perhaps foolishly, I had been assuming that, if anything, the move to New York was Juiceboxxx's one last big attempt at making it. But could it be, I wonder, that while everyone else on the planet moves to New York to chase their dream, Juiceboxxx had come to bury his?

2.

I go through the day imagining how I will carry myself when Juiceboxxx and I meet up. Usually, when I interview people, I'm able to push down my ego completely, and ask questions that make me sound stupid without worrying about what the person I'm talking to thinks of me. This has become easier for me with age, in part because the job I've had for the past three years—writing articles about academic research for a big general interest newspaper—involves interviewing people who always know infinitely more about whatever I'm writing on than I do. This makes it easy to ask everything I need to ask without worrying about impressing anyone.

With Juiceboxxx, I suspect that I won't manage to be so relaxed. I get self-conscious just imagining myself sitting

across from him and asking him questions, and I predict I'm
going to have trouble choosing what expressions to make
with my face. It'll be the first time we've spent significant
time together since that weekend after my freshman year of
college that I mentioned earlier, when I had the idea of putting Juiceboxxx together with a filmmaker friend of mine
named Daniel Kibblesmith. Like me, Daniel had attended
the Cornerstone Church show and been deeply moved by
what he'd seen there. What I wanted was for him to direct
Juiceboxxx's first-ever music video, and after some brain-
storming and negotiations over e-mail, a plan came together.

It so happened that these discussions took place right after
one big hip-hop and R&B station in Chicago announced its
annual outdoor concert, the B96 Summerbash. It was to be
held at a racetrack in a suburb adjacent to Oak Park on the
weekend of August 20, 2004. The lineup included, among
others, Ma$e, who had just un-retired after being a Chris-
tian minister for several years; the Ying Yang Twins, who
had just put out "Wait (The Whisper Song)"; and J-Kwon,
whose single "Tipsy" had recently become a hit. To be honest I don't remember if Juice suggested we get tickets and go
together or if I did, but as soon as it was deemed logistically
viable, it was decided that he would take a bus down from
Milwaukee in time for the show, and then we would film the
video with Daniel the next day.

When Juice sent Daniel an mp3 of the song he wanted to
use, entitled "Thunder Jam #1," Daniel forwarded it to me
right away saying it was every bit as fantastic as he'd hoped.

I was excited but also a little disappointed that Daniel had gotten to hear it before I did.

I still remember sitting at my family's computer and listening to "Thunder Jam #1" for the first time. As the beat came in, Juiceboxxx announced his intention to do the song in one take, then immediately took it back. "That's not gonna happen. That's not a feasible goal," he said. "Maybe thirty takes. Thirty-one? Thirty-two? Thirty-two takes. That's what I'm going for." Then he launched into a friendly but boastful verse in which the most striking line was, "Someday, but probably not / my skills are all I have and I like what I've got."

I played this song over and over that summer, and giggled ecstatically at that opening with my friends Yan and Abe, who were a year younger than me and about to go away to college. They had been blown away by Juiceboxxx that night at Cornerstone too, and had continued listening to *2K3: The Year of the Juice* after I graduated. When Yan got into Oberlin I remember thinking how cool it was that this piece of music was going to be spreading around the country, in part because of me.

Yan and Abe both came to the B96 concert, and while I was obviously closer with them than I was with Juice—Yan was and remains my best friend—I remember trying to play it in my head like "they" were accompanying "us." Throughout the concert Juice danced, jumped around, and foisted copies of *2K3*—what he called "my demo"—to every person willing to take one. His wild bouncing, which revealed an intense enthusiasm for pop music that I didn't understand as well then as I do now, attracted the attention of other concertgoers, some of whom shielded their little kids when Juice got close so that he wouldn't career into them. I remember wondering how apparent it was to these strangers, when they looked at me, Yan, and Abe, that Juice was our leader, and that all we could do was try to keep up with him.

That night Juiceboxxx slept over at my house, and according to him we got drunk together, though all I really remember about it was being over the moon about the fact that we were actually hanging out together.

In the morning we drove my mom's Mazda hatchback over to meet Daniel by my old grade school; according to the treatment Juiceboxxx had written out, the video would begin with him waking up confused and disoriented in an Oak Park playground, and then getting driven back to Milwaukee by me, his friend Leon.

The video turned out really well, I think. In the opening shot, Juice yells, "YO LEON, I'M IN FUCKIN' JOKE PARK! I GOTTA GET OUTTA HERE!" into his phone, while small children run around nearby and parents glance over disapprovingly. In the next shot there's a split-screen of me lying on a couch in my living room, eating ice cream, wearing a bathrobe, and looking very reluctant to drive anyone anywhere.

I'm only providing these details because of how giddy I felt about a) being in the video at all, b) hearing my name come out of Juice's mouth, and c) playing the only guy in Oak Park that Juiceboxxx could count on to come through for him in a time of need. I was proud all over—proud to be behind the wheel, proud that it was my friend Daniel who was in the director's chair, proud that my hometown, not to mention my actual home, was going to get such prominent placement in Juiceboxxx's debut music video.

"Thunder Jam #1," which is still up on YouTube and as of this writing has been viewed more than 23,000 times, ended with Juice hanging out with his Milwaukee friends at a park, while I stood alone near a garbage can with my arms crossed. The idea was—and I'm not totally sure this comes through in the video—that I was waiting for Juice and looking impatiently at my watch before deciding, finally, to let him find his own way home. By the time he realized I was gone ("WHERE THE FUCK IS LEON!?") it was too late. "LEEEEEON!" Juice screams after dialing my number. "PICK UP THE FUCKING PHONE!

Ten years later Yan still says this to me sometimes over Gchat, when he pings me and I'm not at my computer to answer him.

3.

In the afternoon Juice texts me to ask where I'd like to meet. The bars by his sublet in East Williamsburg all look awful, he says apologetically, but he's down to go wherever. Taking the opportunity to assert my status as a local, I tell him I'll think of a place and get back to him, but before I have a chance to do so he writes me again to say that, honestly, he'd almost rather just meet at a Starbucks, if there are any of those in Brooklyn. At first I think this is weird—I can't remember the last time I met up with someone at a Starbucks, especially after dark—but the more I think about it, the more pleased I am with the idea. Sitting and sipping beer with Juiceboxxx in a Brooklyn bar the way I might do with a normal person, I decide, probably wouldn't have felt right anyway.

After making sure he's willing to take the train I tell Juice to meet me outside a subway station about five minutes from my apartment in Brooklyn Heights, where I know there are two Starbucks locations in the immediate vicinity. As I give him the cross-streets and explain how to get there via the G train from Williamsburg I feel guilty knowing that, as an out-of-towner, Juice won't realize how much more convenient this meeting place is for me than it is for him.

A few hours before we're scheduled to meet, I pull out my copy of Juiceboxxx's 2004 release, *R U There God?? It'z Me, Juiceboxxx*. It's a collection of songs that I suspect will sound dated to me if I listened to it now. But at the time of its release, when Juice was on the cusp of graduating from high school, it struck me as a big step forward for him artistically: the cheap-sounding, blippy beats that he rapped over on *2K3* had been upgraded to thicker, more expressive tones, and his rapping, though still quite clumsy, came close to approximating the urgency of his live shows. It was on *R U There God* that Juice first start talking about "thunder"—as in "keep your hands up and keep the beat jamming / we got the th-th-th-th-thunder"—which turned out to be a motif with legs, eventually making its way into the name of his record label, Thunder Zone, and the novelty beverage he later created in order to sell at shows, Thunder Zone Energy.

R U There God also marked the first time that Juice took on a persona that would remain a part of him forever: that of an earnest if somewhat demented motivational speaker. "You gotta listen to what's in your heart / or it might disappear," he wailed on one of the songs. "Follow your dreams / don't live your life in fear / and if those fuckers try to bring you down / say, 'No, I won't give up.' / Just hold your head up high / and rage until you die."

As I listen to the CD for the first time in years, I look at the cover, which shows a teenage Juice perched on his knees against a colorful, neon background. In the picture, he is wearing black jeans and an orange T-shirt, and holding a microphone up to his mouth with a big toothy grimace on his face. It looks like a photo someone took of him during a performance and then cropped rather crudely in Photoshop; I remember Willy telling me that it was influenced by a young, up-and-coming East Coast art collective called Paper Rad that Juice had become friends with through the internet. The Paper Rad aesthetic, which combined bright, Lisa Frank–style colors and shapes with zooming, glitchy graphics reminiscent of Web 1.0, made its way into several of Juice's videos, and his connection to the people who invented it has continued to inform his taste ever since.

It began, Juice would tell me later, when he dropped off

CD-R copies of *2K3* to sell on consignment at a gallery space in Milwaukee called The General Store, where he started going at the age of sixteen to see shows. The General Store, as Juice remembers it, connected Milwaukee to the broader art world, bringing in work by the likes of Paper Rad, Cory Arcangel, and a performance artist named Frankie Martin, who would later become Juice's girlfriend and collaborator.

I remember having some conflicting thoughts about Juice's new relationship with the art world. On the one hand, it seemed like it would be good for his career: With a co-sign from an elite group like Paper Rad, he would gain credibility among a small but potentially influential audience. It would give people who had never heard of him before a reason to take him seriously, insulating him from their first impressions with a layer of protection. At the very least, being associated with artists would earn him a certificate of intentionality, and convince his detractors that insofar as Juice's music sounded bad to them, it sounded that way on purpose.

But there were drawbacks, too, it seemed to me. By having the word "art" branded across his forehead, Juiceboxxx risked undermining the raw, unpracticed energy that had always been his calling card on stage. Intentionality, in other words, cut both ways. If Juice didn't know this when he became interested in contemporary art, he found out the hard way, afterwards, when he lost one of his earliest, and arguably most consequential, champions.

A little background is necessary here: When Juice was

a junior in high school, he started DJing an all-ages dance party in Milwaukee alongside Willy's older brother. The party was held on the first Saturday night of every month, and sometimes there were free cookies, baked by Juice's mom, along with store-bought candy and soda. After about six months, the party had become a hit, at which point a music critic from the *Chicago Reader* named Jessica Hopper went up to Milwaukee and wrote a story about it. In it she called Juiceboxxx "the best DJ to come out of the midwest since Tommie Sunshine." She also said he seemed "unaware of just how good he is," and described him "furiously finessing the records and mixer with long, wiry arms that he's yet to grow into."

It was the first time a music critic of any real stature had written about Juiceboxxx, and according to a blog post Hopper put up on her own website at the time, she was the first person to ever interview him. "He got nervous and developed what looked like hives while we were talking," she wrote, with affection but also obvious pride at having discovered such a young and unformed talent. She mentioned asking Juice to contribute to her feminist zine, and ended the blog post by saying she was going to be bringing him down from Milwaukee to DJ at some event. "Just . . . get ready," she wrote.

About a year after the publication of the profile, Hopper wrote about Juiceboxxx for the *Reader* a second time, this time in the form of a blurb in the calendar section, in connection with a show he was playing at a twenty-one-and-over club called the Empty Bottle. Hopper's opinion of Juice had evidently evolved: the boy she remembered from the summer before as "an earnest, energetic, gentle-natured DJ and performer" had "fallen in with the postironic art-school crowd," she wrote, and as a result, "an act people used to love for its sincerity [was] starting to come off more like a put-on."

I got so mad about this when I read it that I e-mailed an editor at the *Reader* about it, demanding to know what exactly had changed in Hopper's mind since she wrote her hugely positive piece. The answer, it seems clear to me now, was that she had probably become aware of Juice's affiliation with Paper Rad, and didn't like what it implied. She felt played, I'm guessing: the baby savant who had floored her with his guilelessness had turned out to just be another art project.

A decade later, as I sit at my desk and listen to *R U There God*, I wonder what hopes Juice had for it when it came out—whether he thought it was going to get him noticed, get him a record deal, launch him into a Beck-style career as a beloved large-scale weirdo, or what. I think about how, back then, at eighteen years old, Juice wasn't "behind" at all, in terms of how much he had achieved or how likely it was that something really big would happen for him before too long. His future was unwritten then, and as far as he could tell, things were falling into place.

Listening to the record with my grown-up ears, I have to admit that it's not all that surprising that it didn't make

Juiceboxxx a star. While there are a handful of truly excellent songs, each one has at least a few moments that I suspect would make many previously unconverted listeners cringe. Like when he says, "My beats are happening / but I'm not Calvin Johnson." Or when he says, on the record's opening track, "I deliver rhymes better than Pizza Hut / you think that I'm not dope but I just don't give a fuck." And while I know that Juiceboxxx conceived of this silly stuff at the time as a reaction to the self-seriousness that characterized a lot of late-nineties underground rap and punk music, the fact is he had a lot of corny lines, and as I listen to them now, I find it hard to justify the anger I felt at people who dismissed Juiceboxxx as an MC Paul Barman–style jester.

I'd be lying if I said these thoughts never occurred to me at the time. They did. But what I kept coming back to was how Juice had made everyone feel that night at Cornerstone Church—the effect his performance had had on me and my friends, with his gut-level physicality and the sense of chaos he had managed to conjure over the course of just a few minutes. The whole thing was just so undeniable to me. I didn't care that Juiceboxxx lyrics were lame on paper; I had seen what he was truly capable of, and in my eyes it was unimpeachable.

4.

At around seven o'clock I walk to the subway station and lean against a building while I wait for Juice to arrive. As I stand there I try to visualize how I'm going to carry myself when he pops up out of the stairwell—whether I'll shake his hand in a cool way, which would probably feel false, or in the regular way, which could feel too formal and might freak him out. I worry that I'll call him "man" when I first see him, and that I'll end up dropping my g's in that way I hate, and pretend I've heard of things I've never heard of. I resolve, finally, to treat him like some combination of an interview subject who needs to be coaxed into coopera- tion, which he kind of is, and an old friend, even though he really isn't.

After about fifteen minutes I see his tall, lanky frame emerge from the subway landing across the street. He's wearing a windbreaker that's clearly not thick enough to keep him warm in the October chill, which makes me want to yell out to him and run over so we can go indoors as quickly as possible. As he gets his phone out and squints at it, presumably getting ready to call or text me, I try to decide what name to yell out before finally just saying "HEY!" and waving my arms above my head until I get his attention.

He apologizes for being late and I tell him not to worry about it. "Getting here was OK?" I ask. "You've probably gathered by now that the G train is not super-reliable!"

He seems a little dazed and anxious, and when he an- swers me he sounds almost solemn, like a nighttime radio DJ at the end of his shift. He looks at the restaurants and gift shops all around us and says, "This is nice, what's this neighborhood called?" which prompts me to say something self-deprecating about how it's not a very hip area but that, on the plus side, we have not one but two Buckses to choose from. (Unfortunately, I do in fact call them "Buckses," which I never have before in my life, and I hope never to do again.)

When we walk up to the window of the Starbucks closest to us, Juiceboxxx looks in, and after a moment of hesitation says that it looks a little too crowded. "No problem," I say, eager to indulge him as much as I can even though I see a bunch of empty tables, and direct us to the other location instead. When we arrive there Juice says, "Now this is more like it," in a tone of voice that reminds me of Kevin in *Home Alone* when he smells the pizza that's just been delivered to his house and says, "Ah, a lovely cheese pizza, just for me."

After we sit down with our lattes I cut to the chase pretty quickly, clearing my throat and looking down at the table as I start in on the speech I half-prepared on the walk over about why I want to interview and write about him.

"I don't want to make you feel weird right now, but I think you're . . . an inspiring person," I say, struggling to get the words out without stuttering or turning red, or worst of all, sounding insincere. Juice emits a horse-like snort out of the corner of his mouth and looks down at the table. After what feels like ten more minutes of stammering on my part ("I just think you're at this point in your life where . . ."), it becomes clear that I don't really need to talk Juice into anything. To my surprise, he doesn't even qualify his enthusiasm for the idea, or ask how many times I'm envisioning sitting down with him so he can figure out if his schedule allows for it. I had figured at the very least he would ask to approve quotes and stuff, but he doesn't even do that. He's just into it, and I feel even more relieved and excited than I had anticipated.

"All right, then," I say. "Do you mind if I turn on my recorder?"

He says, "Sure, go ahead," without hesitation, and I wonder if his tone is going to suddenly change as soon as I start taping and asking him the questions I've written down in my reporter's notebook. I hope it doesn't, and in service of minimizing the impact, I position the device so that it's not in his immediate field of vision. I think about where to start, what to ask him first, but before I make a decision I find we're already in the middle of things, sipping our drinks as the last remnants of daylight fade away, and talking about the first time he ever played in New York City.

5.

The year was 2005, and the venue was a Williamsburg art gallery that Frankie Martin, whom Juice had recently started dating, had helped book. In the fifty-five-second video of the show that someone uploaded to YouTube you can see that it's light out, and that there are maybe fifteen people standing in the small, well-lit room while Juice performs. He's playing an early entry from the Thunder Jam series—not "Thunder Jam #1," which was the video we made the summer prior, but not "Thunder Jam #8," either, which wouldn't be written for another six years or so. Frankie, meanwhile, is standing off to the side, wearing pigtails under a white beanie and a bright orange hoodie over a striped shirt and green leggings. Her outfit is colorfully clownish but she looks really, really pretty, and you can see she has a digital camera in her hands that she's holding at her chest. As Juice contorts his body, leaping into the air and then whipping his whole torso back and forth as he lands, she smiles and sways to the beat with what looks like real tenderness.

The first time Juice points the microphone into the crowd and calls upon the audience to join him in the triumphant chorus ("Keep your head up and keep the beat slamming! / We got that th-th-th-th-thunder!!!") the reaction is muted, even though everyone's smiling and one guy's even got his arm in the air the way you're supposed to at a hip-hop show. On the second go-round you can see Frankie shout out the words and smile a little self-consciously at whoever is filming the video. As Juice starts the second verse of the song ("Sometimes / I can't decide / should I be brave or should I run and hide? / but I gotta choose bravery / 'cuz a hero is brave / and I was made to be a STAR!"), he whips his shirt off to whoops and cheers, and as he gets down on his knees Frankie lifts her camera to her face and takes a picture.

This was the summer after Juice graduated high school, and he had what felt like real momentum. The electronic music magazine *XLR8R* had published a short article about him headlined "The Next Big Thing." The first *Chicago*

Reader piece had appeared. Most importantly, he was on a real tour for the first time in his life, after playing more than a hundred shows in and around Milwaukee just like the one I had booked for him. The summer of 2005 was different: Juice was performing in basements, galleries, and DIY spaces in cities he had never been to, in front of people he had never met. It was during this period that he began to cement his status as a fixture on the underground rock circuit. Instead of playing alongside other rappers, he played with little-known noise acts with names like Unicorn Hard-On and Men Who Can't Love. The people who went to these shows were almost all white, and for the most part they came expecting to hear guitars, drums, and screaming. Though Juiceboxxx's music didn't always make sense in this context, his spirit did, and in photos from that period you can see people's faces frozen in big, bewildered smiles.

He couldn't have known it at the time, but that summer 2005 tour was Juice's first taste of what would soon become his favorite part of life—the thing he would want to be doing anytime he wasn't doing it, and which would define him, at least in his own mind, and give him a sense of direction. In the meantime, he had to come home, and that fall he enrolled as a freshman at the University of Wisconsin–Milwaukee. He completed two rather miserable semesters and had started his third when something like fate abruptly intervened.

6.

The kid's name was Joe Munz. He was twenty-one, a class-mate of Juice's at UWM, but not someone he'd ever met. Juice was at a friend's apartment when it happened—a duplex in a neighborhood called Riverwest where he often slept on the couch, and where, on this particular Tuesday night, he and his friend were waiting on a couple of sandwiches to arrive from Jimmy John's.

Juice had paid for the sandwiches on the phone with a credit card, and when the doorbell rang and he went down-stairs, he forgot to bring cash with him for the tip. After realizing his mistake he apologized to the delivery boy—he wouldn't learn his name was Joe Munz until it appeared in the *Milwaukee Journal-Sentinel* two days later—and went back up to the apartment to grab his wallet.

When he came back down to the porch, Juice saw a sec-ond man standing on the steps, holding a gun in his hand and demanding that Munz give him all the money he had on him. When Munz resisted the man with the gun shot him at point-blank range, while Juice stood three feet away in shock.

As quickly as he could, Juice ran upstairs to call 9-1-1, and as he made his way up the stairs he heard a second shot. By the time the police arrived the guy with the gun had run off and Munz had collapsed on the porch. "This guy had been sticking up a lot of different Jimmy Johns delivery guys, but this kid was the only one who didn't just give up the money," Juice tells me. "He was a small-town kid. He probably just had a certain level of naïveté or whatever. He tried to fight him off and he died."

This was in October of 2006. Juiceboxxx dropped out of school immediately afterwards, having been convinced by the incident that he didn't have time to do anything with his life that he didn't really want to do. In that mini-documentary I showed to my friend Max, Juice references the murder but declines to say what happened beyond the basic fact that it left him traumatized and inspired him to start booking tours for himself full-time. With that, his life became about riding buses across America, barreling from city to city playing shows and getting paid just enough to get to the next one.

Most likely he would have ended up living that life even if the Munz thing hadn't happened. As Juiceboxxx says, he just has a "chip" in his head that makes him want to be in motion as close to constantly as he can. But it does clarify how, between 2007 and 2010, the positive jams that comprised *R U There God* gave way to black, torn-up songs in which he talked about locking himself in his room and "holding onto a dream that's gone / in a town that time forgot."

7.

"It never occurred to me this was a place where I could actually live," Juice says, when I ask him about his decision to move to New York. "Somehow it always just seemed unattainable for me to live here, I guess because I was just too much of a spazz. For years I was like, 'I can live in Milwaukee and pay next to nothing in rent and jump in a van with another band or jump on a Greyhound bus and tour and come home with a little bit of money in my pocket.' And that just seemed ideal, and I figured if something would happen I'd take it from there."

During this period, which lasted almost five years, Juice paid an average of two hundred dollars per month in rent, occasionally relying on his roommates to cover for him. For a normal show he would earn at least fifty to one hundred dollars, he tells me, plus whatever he took in at the merch table. But by 2007 and 2008, he was getting occasional bookings at lucrative college shows and opening slots for bigger artists like Madlib. These would net him between $1,000 and $1,500 per show—huge sums, compared to what he was used to, which he would stretch out for months by eating frozen pizzas, taking public transportation everywhere, and resolutely refusing, unlike many of his friends, to start smoking cigarettes or weed.

Finally being in New York, Juice says, is exciting to him, especially after living in Los Angeles without a car, where his commute to the practice space where he rehearsed with his band took ninety minutes, and involved two buses, a train, and two miles of walking. In New York, he says, everything's so close, and it's so easy to see everyone, even if they live in, like, Far Rockaway, where a bunch of his artist and musician friends share a house. Unlike Los Angeles, New York strikes him as hospitable to "alternative lifestyles."

As I listen to this, I can't help but think that Juice's image of New York is totally romantic and has no connection to reality—that he's imagining some old version of the city where creative, free people can roam and live on nothing, spending their days collaborating with each other on fanciful projects, never knowing or really worrying about where their food money is going to come from.

"What's funny is I'm constantly reading articles by like, old school New Yorkers about how the city has changed, blah, blah, blah, and how it sucks now," Juice says, as if reading my mind. Earlier that day, he says, he saw an article by David Byrne saying that if the city got any more gentrified, he was going to move and never come back. "To me that's just hot air," he says. "People forget how good they have it here."

Before I have time to wonder whether this means I'm just jaded, or worse, sheltered and missing out on the actual beating heart of New York, Juice brings up a show he played on a dumpy block of Bushwick one summer long ago with an avant-garde punk band called Japanther, and how that neighborhood feels like a college campus now—his point being that he's not naïve and that he knows New York changes quickly, but still believes it's the most exciting place in the world.

"I was at that show," I say, barely concealing my pride at this fact, and picturing in my head the too-tight Japanther shirt I bought afterwards despite having never heard of them before.

"Oh, yeah, you were," Juice says, but I wonder if he really remembers.

When I ask him how he's making rent now, he explains that the only reason he could afford to leave Milwaukee and spend this month in New York is that he got paid $8,000 for writing a jingle that ended up being used in a Microsoft ad. This had become his business model in recent years, he explains: just doing "weird little gigs," like writing the theme song for a children's television show or getting commissioned to do remixes for random Japanese bands.

The Microsoft ad came about because of a guy Juice knows at a firm that hires musicians to do fairly lucrative commercial work. And while the money he made off that is the main thing keeping Juice solvent, he's also been helping out around the offices of a record label run by his friend Dre Skull, doing stuff like uploading YouTube videos and mailing out packages. It's a little weird for him, I can tell, because just a few years ago, when Juice was in his dance-rap phase, this guy Dre Skull was one of his main musical collaborators. Since then he has apparently found real success as a label-owner and producer, scoring a big notch on his belt by putting out an album by a guy Juice tells me is "the Lil Wayne of Jamaica," and more recently, producing a bunch of songs on Snoop Dogg's reggae album.

I wonder to myself: Why didn't Dre Skull offer to put out *I Don't Wanna Go into the Darkness*? Did he not think it was good enough? I'm sure Juice didn't ask, or expect him to offer, but he would have to be inhuman not to have at least thought about it.

Dre Skull is not the only one of Juice's longtime friends who has broken out in one way or another. But for everyone who has achieved even a modicum of success, like that guy Corndawg he was talking to Max about the other night, ten others have quit or resigned themselves to doing music as a hobby and nothing more.

"A lot of my friends are like, 'Yeah, I'm done, I don't care about playing,'" Juice says. "And in a way that's the, like, logical, right thing to do when you're twenty-seven or twenty-eight—to say, 'yeah, I'm kinda over this . . . I've had some fun but I don't really see a future in this.' Sometimes I try to say that shit but I feel like I'm just fucking kidding myself. It doesn't feel cool to say I still want to just fucking tour. But for some reason I still have this total, one hundred percent desire to just, like, play."

The upcoming tour, he tells me, will begin on November 1 with a show in Ithaca. The van, which he and his band are renting, will seat Juice, Willy, and their new drummer Mike, plus the "cyber punk" duo Extreme Animals, and a DJ from Baltimore named Schwarz whom Juice regards as a kindred spirit. After Ithaca they'll go to Boston, Providence, and New Haven, and then come back to Brooklyn on the fifth to play at a place in Bushwick called the Passion Lounge. From there they will drive to the Midwest for five dates that include Milwaukee, then up to Toronto, and then back east. I put the Passion Lounge show in my calendar in my phone as soon as he mentions it because I already know there's no way I'm going to miss it.

These shows will be Juice's first in more than a year, he says, with the exception of a few small ones he did while he was staying in Milwaukee. When I ask him why it's been so long, he explains that ditching his iPod in favor of a live band a few years back has made it logistically hard for him to tour as much as he wants to, because now that he relies on other people, he can no longer just pick up and hit the road at the drop of a hat like he used to.

When I ask him why he doesn't just go back to doing it the old way, at least occasionally, he says his music has just changed too much since the early days, and that his vision for the show he wants to put on now depends too much on live drums and live guitar. What he wants to do, he says, is make "truly American music" that combines everything he loves about rap and rock, without compromising on it just because some terrible bands from the late nineties poisoned the well.

"So you must be really looking forward to starting the tour," I say, feeling for the first time all night like a rock journalist interviewing a celebrity.

"Absolutely. I can't wait," he replies, kind of sounding like one.

When I ask him what he likes about it, why it's fun for him, I figure maybe he'll talk about the camaraderie of van life or something like that, giving me a chance to hear some fun tour stories. Instead all he says is that he just loves traveling with a purpose.

"Nothing beats having a real mission. To put it on the line every night, just give it one hundred percent? I know it seems like, sort of inconsequential. But just to be able to travel and play a show, to actually touch ground, that matters to me," he says. "I want to fucking cover the earth."

When we wrap up I point him toward the subway and we agree to talk again soon. I walk home feeling more enthralled with him than ever, floored at how ambitious he sounds and marveling at the amount of confidence he's capable of holding in his brain alongside all the hopelessness.

3

GENIUS VS. CRITIC

I.

When I was in college, my best friends and I had a game we liked to play in which we divided people into "geniuses" and "critics." We didn't use these words literally, but as shorthand for concepts that preoccupied us, and which we wanted to have at our fingertips for easy deployment. Under our definition, a "genius" was someone so certain about what it was that made them special that they could move through the world with an un-self-conscious sense of purpose—someone who couldn't help but be the way they were, and had original, immaculate visions that poured out of them as if by magic. "Critics," meanwhile, were calculated and careful—people who conducted their lives with effortful competence, but in the end could do nothing more than react to the geniuses in their midst.

Though I didn't start using these terms until college, I can say, in retrospect, that I spent much of my adolescence wishing I could stop feeling like a "critic" and discover a hidden "genius" under all my dull neuroses. I maintained this hope for years, and coveted a way of being natural and self-contained that seemed to animate everyone I thought was cool. This included a few famous people I was excited by—obvious ones, like Kurt Cobain—but I felt it most strongly when spending time around some of the more amazing actual people I was fortunate enough to know.

There was a guy who lived across town from me named Gabe, a stocky stoner with messy jet-black hair, about four years my senior, whose capacity to be imaginative and hilarious in conversation wowed me in the same way I would later be wowed by Lil Wayne's ability to make up entire songs on the fly. I became friends with Gabe when I was sixteen and he was twenty, maybe a year before I met Juiceboxxx. Gabe and I communicated mainly over IM, except for a handful of times when I went over to the apartment where he lived with his parents. During one of my visits to his house I smoked pot with him, my first time ever; Gabe sent me home with a skull-shaped bowl that he no longer used and which I hid in an old sock that my mom found almost immediately.

Most of my conversations with Gabe involved him showing me funny things from the Internet—he posted on obscure message boards and had interests that led him into corners of the web I never explored—and talking to me about his favorite movies, books, and music. I can say now, with the benefit of hindsight, that Gabe appealed to me in the same way Willy did, in that he was an obviously brilliant audodidact, and loved all kinds of things, like wrestling and violent cartoons, that I associated, thanks to my parents, with low culture. Before we became friends, I didn't really know such people existed; in my mind, being smart automatically meant enjoying only rarefied, classic art, and doing all your homework so that you could get into a top-ranked college. I believed this because my parents believed it, and when I encountered Gabe I remember thinking, for what might have been the first time in my life, that I was seeing greatness in someone whose intelligence and taste would not be legible to them. This experience shook something loose in me, and made me realize that the world was full of stuff that I could like and be moved by without anyone's permission.

I'd like to think I would have eventually had that breakthrough anyway. But Gabe catalyzed it, and in the process introduced me to an entirely new value system for understanding culture—a value system that would later dovetail very nicely with, and probably intensify, my love for Juiceboxxx.

What this value system said, essentially, was that true art had to be visceral, not cerebral, and that real rock and roll, especially, came not from the brain but from "the crotch." Gabe saw inherent virtue in authenticity, and privileged raw, high-energy performance over all other forms of expression.

His theory of art was one that, like the genius/critic idea that I would embrace a few years later, rewarded an ability to channel, with brawny originality, the primitive forces running through one's body, and turn them into style.

It sounded entirely convincing to sixteen-year-old me, even if it left me no choice but to believe that I'd been living my life up to that point as an irredeemable dork. And while I couldn't just suddenly stop wanting to impress my teachers, or being nervous around girls, or liking soft-as-a-blanket indie bands like the Shins and Modest Mouse, I took Gabe's ideas very much to heart, and committed myself to becoming a person he would be proud to know. To that end I bought *Raw Power* by the Stooges, read Jack Kerouac novels, and tried to write columns for the school newspaper that sounded like the manic prose of Lester Bangs.

As much as I wanted to love *Raw Power*, though, the devastating reality was that I pretty much never felt like listening to it. And as badly as I wished I could be a live wire like Dean Moriarty from *On the Road*, I secretly identified much more intensely with that book's worried narrator, the restrained and helplessly middle-class Sal.

Only Juiceboxxx made me feel like I could live up to the standards I had set for myself by way of Gabe's teachings. Here was a bone fide "genius," an Iggy Pop–like dynamo, whose energy affected me in the way I had come to believe all great art was supposed to—whose presence made my blood pressure rise.

I wasn't the only one who reacted to Juiceboxxx this way.

It was, in fact, invariably what people who saw him live talked about when they tried to explain why he was good. This was true going all the way back to that "Next Big Thing" article in *XLR8R*, in which the author declared that Juice's "genius lies in his honesty, his lightheartedness, his youth, and [his] absence of irony," and Jessica Hopper's first *Reader* piece, which said "his sincerity may be what's most striking."

Generally when people talk about things like "sincerity" and the "absence of irony," what they're reacting to is enthusiasm that strikes them as trustworthy—enthusiasm powered by unfiltered, joyful energy that invites the beholder to take it at face value without having to wonder about whether the person radiating it has ulterior motives. With Juiceboxxx, this has been a central talking point in part because his early stuff, especially, was so easy to reasonably mistake for novelty rap, and it was crucial for him and the people who liked him to get the message across—if only half-convincingly—that he really wasn't joking around. That's why in all those early articles there are also squirming quotes from Juice where he says defensive things like, "I want it to be known that I am not ironic or mocking hip-hop."

But there's another, more important reason that Juiceboxxx's exceptional sincerity is so often held up as his central virtue, which is that when you watch him play live, the main thing you pick up on is that he appears fully invested in and committed to what he's doing, and also that he looks almost feral as he's doing it. He is what you might call "pure id": a lightning bolt of a human being who looks to be in free fall, and who is authentically himself in a way that most people—again, including me—just don't know how to be.

Being able to recognize and respond to Juice's talent wasn't just thrilling to me because of how good he was. It also gave me reason to hope that, despite not liking the Stooges, I was capable of responding in the right way to high-octane, authentic art. True, Juiceboxxx's lyrics were self-conscious and sometimes too clever in a way that I knew Gabe would not approve of. But that almost made my reaction to his live show that much more trustworthy: here was a guy you needed to see in the flesh in order to understand. Then there was the fact that Juiceboxxx had succeeded in attracting Frankie Martin, the beautiful girl associated with Paper Rad who became his girlfriend when she was in her late twenties and he was just eighteen. Though I'm somewhat embarrassed by this, I have to admit that Frankie's interest in Juice confirmed my feeling that, clever lyrics or not, he had something undeniable to offer—something primal that no one could resist when they came face to face with it. I imagined Frankie seeing Juice live for the first time and being shot through with desire, then coming up to him after his set and taking him by complete surprise by showing interest in him.

For all these reasons, I saw Juiceboxxx as an exemplar of Gabe's "crotch" model of rock and roll, which simultaneously made me more sure that I was right to be captivated by him, and also more confident that the "crotch" model itself was correct. The fact that I usually couldn't feel it deep down,

I concluded, didn't mean the value system was wrong—just that I had not yet become capable of living up to it.

2.

Now that it's been a few years, I can say my friends and I might have been overthinking it a bit with the whole genius/critic thing. All we were really saying, I think, was that some people have the souls of artists and others don't. And while that's arguably not a trivial observation, it no longer strikes me as all that revelatory, except insofar as it helped each of us determine which side of the divide we were on.

I for one had spent much of my life thinking that, although it was clear I had not yet found my calling, I could and would still turn out to be some kind of artist. What kind, I didn't really know, but rather than being discouraged by this, I let it have the paradoxical effect of making it easier to believe it would happen—that all I had to do was figure out what my talents predisposed me to and the rest would come naturally. Even as I did what I had to do in order to ensure my future prosperity—studying for the SATs, enrolling in extracurricular activities like mock trial and French club—I operated under the only-sometimes conscious assumption that none of it would ultimately be necessary when I discovered my artistic gifts and made them the basis of my livelihood. Despite getting older and older and being no closer to knowing what it was I had to say to the world, I stayed optimistic about the possibility of eventually getting there.

Then one day I stopped. And while I would never blame it on Juiceboxxx, it is nevertheless true that the change came as a direct result of me crossing paths with him when I did.

I was a sophomore at Harvard when it happened. Juice was playing a show in someone's dorm room at BU, and I was there alone, because as usual none of my friends would go with me. Watching him from the back of the room, I was in awe of his energy, as I had been the half dozen times I'd seen him play up to that point. This time, though, something was different: For the first time ever, I found myself trying to think in concrete terms about what it was he was actually doing up there that someone like me wasn't capable of. I pictured myself in his place as I watched him; imagined what it would feel like to move the way he was moving, make the faces he was making, utter the guttural sounds that were coming from the pit of his stomach. Afterwards, as I walked home I made a deeply embarrassing decision that I have never told anyone about, and have not forgotten even though I really wish I could: I too would become a rapper, and like Juiceboxxx, I would wow everyone who saw me with my genius.

It would be easy, I thought to myself. All I'd have to do was think of a funny stage name, write a bunch of amusing rhymes, buy a jumpsuit like the one I remembered Juice wearing at the church show, and book myself a slot in the basement where Harvard's student bands performed every Thursday night. I imagined myself jumping around frenetically and pouncing on people, bending my body at sharp angles and having my eyes bulge out of my skull so that I looked unhinged and a little dangerous. I would grab audience members and rap at them, and then I would end my set in a ball on the floor, panting and growling.

I figured Juiceboxxx wasn't nearly famous enough for anyone to realize where I was getting my moves. I imagined my friends and classmates watching me, still and stunned, as I transformed before their eyes into a possessed, unsettling creature and overwhelmed them with my unbridled intensity.

Thinking of this fantasy today makes me sick to my stomach, and I consider it a great stroke of luck that my intentions evaporated before I could take any concrete steps toward realizing them. And though it's hard to say now whether it was giving up on this pitiful plan, or hatching it in the first place, that decisively snuffed out any hope I still had at that point of becoming a person who created art, I nevertheless feel confident saying that the profound self-loathing that filled me afterwards changed the way I thought of myself. Like a person waking up from a painfully revealing anxiety dream, I had glimpsed a part of myself that was deeply shameful. Worse, I had let it take over my thoughts for long enough to start thinking of possible names I could perform under, and to actually picture myself on stage. It was the ultimate "critic" move: with no original instincts of my own, all I could think to do was try to copy someone else's.

3.

What tortures me about that story, which Juiceboxxx will only learn about if and when he reads this, is that in the beginning, my dreams of tapping into some fount of artistic creativity deep inside of myself were mostly pure. As a small child, I painted and drew pictures; later, as a sixth grader, I wrote melodramatic short stories and chapter books about talking animals, and in high school I even composed a novella about a group of friends hanging out together as counselors at a summer camp.

Of all my experiments, though, none held my attention as long or with as much intensity as my attempts to make music, which began when I was eight years old, and continued, on and off, until the end of my freshman year of college.

I'm reminded of this, every once in a while, when I search for something in my iTunes and accidentally come upon a recording of myself as a teenager, singing and playing a song that I wrote, with a band behind me that I was responsible for putting together. It feels impossible now that it was really me, and the fact that it was—that for approximately twelve years of my life, my most deeply held ambition was to become a great songwriter—is somehow reassuring to me. Granted, there's something pathetic about a twenty-eight-year-old looking back to when he was literally a third grader and being impressed with his ingenuity and drive, but I can't help it: at that age, I was filling notebooks with melodies expressed in a musical notation of my own invention, and recording entire albums by setting up a series

of tape-decks next to each other and playing different instruments into them one by one in order to layer them on
top of one another. I pounded on books and bags full of
change to approximate drums and cymbals. I used scissors
and glue to make liner notes with track lists and covers that
had my face on them. I called myself, no joke, "The Terrorist
of Humanity."

The first proper band I was ever in was called Section 69,
which formed in middle school. My bandmates were Nigel,
a close friend I competed with over who could collect more
Nirvana bootlegs, and Evan, the guy who would eventually
go on to start Wrong Turn and, thanks to my curatorial vision, play on the same bill as Juiceboxxx.

The first and best of the eight songs I wrote for Section
69 was called "Punk Mentality," and it was all about how
confused I was about various aspects of punk-rock culture.
The first verse went, "What the hell does 'DIY' mean? / And
how about a 'zine'? / This fucking punk mentality / all these
words I've seen."

Nigel and I performed an acoustic version of the song
in our second period guitar-playing class at school. The
teacher told me, when I asked, that it would be OK if there
was swearing in the lyrics. Afterwards, Nigel and I passed
around a four-song tape we recorded on a boombox my
mom had bought at a garage sale; we called it "The Lauda-
num EP," after a type of drug I found out about by flipping
to a random page in the dictionary, and for some reason the
cover was adorned with the face of a "creepy" clown.

Around the same time Section 69 was coming together, Nigel and I started something we referred to as a record label called Underage Records. We had a Geocities page with an "upcoming releases" section full of hypothetical albums that never saw the light of day, and at school I'd fill notebooks with sketches of potential album art. The apex of the label's existence came when we "put out" a cassette compilation entitled "Juvenile Hall." There was a baby on the cover, which I printed along with the liner notes on the color printer at my dad's office at the University of Illinois. The tape included one song by Section 69 and one by Nigel's other band, Gloss. The rest of it was split between terrible songs by bands I'd contacted through unsigned-artists.com, and a few pretty good ones that Nigel's cousin, who ran an actual record company in Normal, Illinois, let us use for free.

After Section 69 broke up, my musical career pretty much stalled until I met Willy, who inspired me to download recording software onto my computer, and Juiceboxxx, whose performance at Cornerstone made me want to start a new band, called The Godzz.

The Godzz consisted of an older guy named Ian on drums, a cool girl named Cindy, whom I'd known since fifth grade, on guitar, and a quiet freshman from my school named Miles on bass. I was the lead singer. Naturally I made a shamefully big deal about the correct spelling of Godzz whenever I told people about it. And yes, my first instinct was to follow Juiceboxxx's lead and have three Zs, not two, but that seemed to evoke sleepiness rather than the raw rock-and-roll energy we were planning to deliver.

Unfortunately, organizing and promoting our first show—which was to be held not at Cornerstone, but another teen-friendly Unitarian church in Joke Park—was where most of my efforts as lead singer of the Godzz were directed. All told, we only got to practice together three times before the big day came, and even more unfortunately, our set consisted entirely of covers because we hadn't bothered to write our own material. It pains me to write this now, but we opened with "Blitzkrieg Bop" by the Ramones and "Keep on Rockin' in the Free World," and closed with extended versions of "Roadrunner" and "Sister Ray." We were awful. My singing was awful. Everyone in the room stayed seated the entire time, and afterwards I overheard some guy saying that the band itself wasn't too bad but that they'd have to get rid of the vocalist if they ever wanted to get anywhere.

It was a horrible experience and the only reason I didn't go home immediately after we played was that I wanted to collect our share of the door, which we were splitting evenly with the rest of the bands on the bill even though it was obvious to everyone involved how little work we'd put into our performance and how little we deserved to be paid anything.

In the wake of that fiasco I decided to get serious—to start writing songs and recording them on my computer, just like Willy did. During this time I would rush home after school so as to have as much time as possible to spend on recording before my mom came home. When I finished a song I would send it to Willy for appraisal, and rejoice whenever he told me that one of them was good.

Eventually, I got the Godzz together to learn the songs, and later we recorded them, under a new, more dignified name, with the help of a semi-professional engineer who was friends with our drummer. The result was a six-song CD that still occupies prime real estate in my heart. Despite the fact that I have not self-identified as a "musician" in years—that I never did, to tell the truth, even though I wanted to—I continue to think the songs are well written, if not particularly well performed or well produced. And sometimes I can't help but wonder what might have happened if I hadn't lost interest, or given up, or done whatever it was I did that resulted in me eventually giving my guitar away to a mover.

4.

As much as I loved writing and recording music, it was a bitter given to me all through my childhood that my parents did not share my enthusiasm, and when the subject came up, they let me understand in no uncertain terms that I was wasting my time. Meanwhile, everyone else I knew who was into music seemed to have moms and dads who were excited by their kids' desire to play music—who, from the outside at least, seemed to interpret their impulses charitably, as the early stirrings of significant, possibly consequential passions. Evan, for instance, who is now a professional trombone player, had a dad who was almost always willing to drive him to practice and sometimes even helped us carry his drum kit in and out of my house. Nigel's dad, meanwhile, had his own punk band, the Laughing Boys, that played shows around town and owned a cache of effect pedals that Nigel was allowed to borrow whenever he wanted. I remember Evan's mom even listened to the four-song cassette tape that Section 69 recorded in my living room while my mom wasn't home, and commented positively on it—something about how, while she was initially somewhat put off by the amount of swearing in the lyrics, it was clear that the songs called for it because they were so emphatic. I remember thinking this was incredibly generous of her.

My parents, on the other hand, wouldn't even let me buy myself an electric guitar until I was in seventh grade, a full year after I started asking for one. That fall, when my dad dropped me off for my first lesson, he looked at all the band stickers I'd affixed to my brand new guitar case and said, in a tone of voice that I'm sure he didn't expect me to remember for the rest of my life, "You know, when your new teacher meets you, he will see these stickers, and he will know right away that the only reason you are here is that you want to be like somebody else."

Some time later, after my parents got divorced, I told my dad while we were driving to my grandmother's house that I wanted to play him a tape I had made called "The Horoscope EP." The tape, which I'd brought with me in my pocket, was decorated with a graphite sketch, drawn by me, of something approximating a crystal ball, and had four songs on it that I'd recorded on my computer with just an acoustic guitar. The first and best of these was about staring at a girl named Lauren in my social studies section ("Sit behind you in class / Can't wait for you to turn around / your hair looks pretty from here / wonder what you're doing now"), and despite the childish lyrics I still believe it was a beautiful song. When I put it on that day in the car I remember shaking with nervousness as the opening chords played and my dad listened. I had no idea whether he was going to sit through the whole thing and then react, or what; there had been plenty of times when things I'd played for him in the car had prompted him to simply hit the stop button without warning. In this case, to my disappointment as well as my relief, he weighed in early, during the first chorus, as he examined the cover art while sitting at a red light. "Listen," he said, not without warmth, "it's fine that you are doing this. But you have to ask yourself: is it really the thing you are better at than other people?"

He was right, of course, and I'm glad he said it. Looking back on it now, I sincerely believe that his honesty was exactly what I needed, and when I have kids of my own I fully intend to be just as frank with them about what they are and aren't good at. At the time it stung, of course, but in the way something only can when you know it's true.

5.

Eventually, I learned to keep to myself the depth of my desire to write songs and play in bands, figuring that the gulf between me and my parents was too vast for them to ever see these were things worth pursuing. This gulf, as I realized only later, was not just generational but cultural: my parents had brought me to the United States from Moscow at the age of five, and many of their ideas about how a young man should spend his time were informed by a set of values rooted in their own Soviet upbringing that were simply incommensurate with the life of an American teenager.

It was those values that led my parents to have what I think were unusually specific hopes for what kind of person I would turn out to be, as well as some very specific fears about how I might go wrong. Their agenda—and I use that word neutrally, as I think parents absolutely should have agendas when it comes to raising their kids—went beyond simply wanting me to do well in school and getting into a good college. What they wanted was for me to be interested in things worth being interested in—for me to be a lively, engaged person who was fun to talk to, and who could appreciate the art, poetry, and novels they believed to be the greatest in the world.

I don't blame them for worrying about me. After all, as a young American-in-training, I lived in a totally different universe than the one they'd been raised in, and they must have known it was inevitable I would be influenced by it in profound ways no matter how hard they worked on me at

home. At the heart of the problem was that American culture, by and large, struck them as crude and vulgar, and the
fact that I was so drawn to it—that I liked Nirvana instead
of Bach, that I cared more about watching TV and listening
to the radio than I did about reading literature or going to
museums—left them dismayed and regretful. The problem
was not just my taste, at least not in the narrow sense of the
word. Rather, it was about how I wanted to spend my time
and what I gravitated toward when left to my own devices.
At stake was not just what I liked and didn't like—it was the
sum total of my natural inclinations.

And so they pushed back, undertaking an educational
campaign that, to their credit, did result in me reading a
bunch of important books and seeing a whole lot of classic
movies, but also left our relations somewhat frayed, and my
feelings frequently hurt. One day in eighth grade, my dad
came to my school to give a presentation about what he did
as a biology professor. Afterwards, a kid named Michael
whom I considered to be a huge loser came up to him and
started asking him questions about his work, while I sat in
the back of the room and waited, out of earshot. I watched
as my dad sat down with a notebook and sketched something with a pencil before tearing out the piece of paper and
giving it to Michael to keep. Later, when we were walking to
his car, my dad asked me who that boy was, and why wasn't
I friends with him, and why didn't I ever ask him such interesting questions. "He had a real glint in his eye," I remember
my dad saying. "Where is yours?"

6.

I should be clear: It wasn't that my parents didn't like America, or that they believed I would have turned out better if I'd been raised in Moscow. They also didn't mean to discourage me. They just had a very strong faith in the distinction between high and low culture—one that didn't make sense here but had been absolutely essential in the Soviet Union, because it separated people like my parents and their friends from the millions of ordinary Russians who believed in the Communist party and embraced the worthless culture that emerged from it. Even as a child I understood that being part of the group my parents belonged to—a largely Jewish, highly educated circle of people who prized intellect above all else and despised the Soviet regime—meant being both an underdog and a member of the elite. In that context, being able to distinguish between high and low culture was not just a matter of preference. It defined the kind of person you were at your very core.

In the America I was growing up in, it just wasn't like that, and this was difficult for my parents to get used to. As far as they were concerned, there was what "everyone" liked, and then there was what discerning people liked, and they wanted very badly for me to be discerning. This, I think, informed their aggressive, highly focused approach to raising me, and explains why they considered it deeply disappointing that all I seemed to be interested in doing was watching music videos on MTV, attending crowded rock concerts, and spending all my money on CDs.

Juiceboxxx, I believe, is the embodiment of everything my parents could never understand about American culture. From the way he talks (a lot of "man" and "like" and tons of gratuitous swearing) to the way he dresses (colorfully, sloppily), he is the image of "shpana," a Russian word that translates roughly to "thuggish punk," and which my mom loved to invoke in describing kids she didn't want me to hang out with. Every morning in middle school she and I would fight about my baggy jeans, which she said made me look like a "gangster," until one day, in order to prove to her that all my classmates, not just the dirty monsters, wore baggy pants, I brought a camera into school and took pictures of people's legs during lunch. "It proves nothing," my mom said when I got the film developed and showed her. "Anyone can go out in the street and find a bunch of idiots."

This was why I never told her, or my dad, about Juice, or tried to explain to them why he mattered to me. The one night he slept over at my house—this was during the summer after my freshman year, when I was helping him shoot that music video in Oak Park—I snuck him in and out the back door in order to avoid making introductions, because I knew for a fact that my mom would take one look at him and get mad that I was hanging out with such a plainly inappropriate person. And while my mom's attitude has softened with time—as did my dad's, in the year or two before he died in 2006—I nevertheless am confident that if she were forced to watch him perform, she would physically fight her way out of the venue.

A few days after Juice and I have our first dinner in New York, I'm talking to my mom on the phone and I mention to her, when she asks what I've been up to, that I recently met up with a musician I knew a little bit back in high school whom I'm planning to write an article about. I regret bringing it up as soon as I do: considering I have a hard enough time summarizing for my peers why I find Juiceboxxx so magnetic, doing it for my mother seems basically impossible. Nevertheless I give it my best shot, starting by telling her he was a friend of Willy, whom she met the one time he stayed at our house.

"He was the funny rocker who never took his hat off, right?" my mom says, with an openness in her voice that catches me off guard. It makes me remember how touched I was by the warm welcome she gave Willy when he visited, despite being somewhat horrified when I came home from a summer camp for gifted students having found the one guy there who wasn't planning to go to college.

"And did I ever meet this other boy?" she asks.

"No," I say.

"What kind of music does he make?"

"It's . . . a mix between rap and rock," I say hesitantly, knowing that I'm about to lose her interest or, worse, make her mad at me.

Instead she laughs, in a friendly, tender way that seems to reflect the trust she has gradually built up in my judgment over the years. "Well, you know it's not my piece of cake, but . . ."

"Cup of tea," I correct her. "But yeah, I know. The problem is that he's not most people's cup of tea."

"Oh," she says. "So you mean he is not a very popular musician?"

"No, not really."

"Hm. But you think he is interesting, right?"

"Right."

"Well, then, that's great," she says. "If you think he's interesting and no one else does, to me that is a good sign."

Soon after we say our goodbyes and hang up, and I feel incredibly relieved, and acutely conscious of just how much I love my mom.

Later, as I'm closing my eyes to go to sleep, it occurs to me that as different as Juiceboxxx and I are, it seems he and I have arrived at a very similar point in our lives for what might be the first time ever: no longer kids, no longer even all that young, we are both coming to terms with what we are and what we are not. Where I, like many, used to dream of becoming an artist, I have instead turned out to be a professional: a reporter with a solid career writing feature stories for a newspaper. Juice, meanwhile, seems to be taking stock of all the comfort and stability he's given up by committing himself to his art, and trying to figure out if he can keep on doing it—and what he'll do if he can't—as he gets closer and closer to being a thirty-year-old man.

4

STUPID, STUPID, STUPID

I.

The next time Juiceboxxx and I meet up, it's for dinner at a Mexican restaurant, where I make a modest show of paying for his burrito because, as I tell him half-jokingly, "that's how it works when a journalist writes about someone." Over the course of our conversation—during which I try to get him to draw a through-line for me from his early days playing with punk bands in the Midwest, to his dance music phase, to his recent decision to try and resuscitate rap rock—he talks a lot about instinct.

"My life has been an exercise in following my gut," he says at one point, "and that's led me to some really weird places. But you know, I feel like I owe it to myself to see certain things through. And I feel like I've been building something. And it's hard for me to know what the end-point is."

After more prodding, he kind of throws his hands up. "I don't know, man, I can't stress this enough—when it comes to actually how I started doing this and why I keep doing it, it's been a hundred percent natural."

As a journalist trying to make sense of Juice's life, I find these answers extremely unsatisfying. But the fact of the matter is the things he's saying are perfectly consistent with my longstanding impression of him as a person who became what he is without ever deciding to—a person who, unlike me and most everyone I'm friends with, seems capable of existing in a mode that is totally spontaneous and uncalculated.

I ask Juice to describe how he wants audiences to react to him when they're watching him perform. His answer is straightforward: what he wants is for people to get as intensely physical as he himself is when he's on stage. The goal, in other words, is to coax people into turning themselves up to his frequency, and make them capable of matching his energy even though, in their normal lives, they can't even come close, and are never moved to try.

What usually ends up happening, as I know from attending Juiceboxxx shows in Illinois, Wisconsin, Massachusetts, and New York, is that this works on some people and not on others. While some audience members are instantly turned off, a few can be counted on to take obvious pride in really throwing themselves into it—to dance really, really hard and thrash around as if to make clear that they appreciate what Juice is doing on a deeper, more immediate level than everybody else in the room.

Maybe I'm projecting. But if I am, it's not because I tend to be one of those people. In fact, I never have been, because for all the times I've heard that I should "dance like no one's watching," it just does not come naturally to me, no matter how badly I'd like it to. Instead of setting me free, like I know it's supposed to, dancing just makes me feel like a fraud— like I'm performing a part, badly, that was written for somebody else. Part of the problem might be that it strikes me as deranged and unethical to be moving around in ways that basically force the people in my immediate vicinity to imagine me having sex. The rest is that it's just not in me, just like loving "Raw Power" isn't in me, as if I'm missing the receptors necessary to truly connect with music and with other people using nothing but my "body."

As you can see, I can't even use that word without putting scare quotes around it. It just feels gross to me, and reminds me, in an ironically visceral way, of how left out I have always felt in situations in which I was invited to undergo some physically transcendent collective experience. Among them, off the top of my head: watching a Pink Floyd laser show at the Adler Planetarium for my ninth birthday and mostly just feeling normal; going to Spa Castle, the three-story sauna-and-hot-tub relaxation mecca in Queens, and mostly just feeling normal. Also, going to a Fiona Apple concert after reading a million articles about how incredible she was live, and walking home afterwards utterly disappointed in myself for appreciating the performance but mostly . . . just feeling normal.

It has been sharpest at dance parties, though, which I have been attending, stubbornly, for the past ten years and almost never enjoying as much as the people around me. This wouldn't be that big of a deal—I would have just stopped going to these things and not worried about it—except that the past ten years have coincided with the blossoming of an idea in American youth culture that held dancing up as the biggest deal in the world. According to this idea—which takes Gabe's "crotch" theory of rock and roll and broadens it as far as it'll go—the inability to dance one's face off is nothing less than a failure of personality: evidence, essentially, of a shriveled up, cold, and boring soul. Maybe it was always seen that way. But if it was, I felt insulated from it for much of my childhood, and felt no amount of shame about not wanting to gyrate, or shake my hips, or whatever, until around 2004 or 2005, when seemingly every influential, youth-oriented media outlet started enthusiastically covering "dance punk" bands like the Rapture and LCD Soundsystem. These bands were saviors come to rescue America's indie rock fans from their closed-off, head-bobbing, flannel-wearing selves, was the message—and they were going to show us how to really have a good time. More to the point, they were going to teach us how to get in touch with the parts of ourselves that really mattered, but which we couldn't gain access to on our own because we were disgusting, sexless geeks.

I remember feeling, throughout college and afterwards, like I had to be on board with this stance if I wanted to be modern and enlightened. But as hard as I tried to make myself enjoy dancing, I couldn't. Rather than set me free, or whatever it was supposed to do, it tended to make me feel like I was expressing the opposite of my true self. In fact, in many situations I can remember, it felt like psychological torture.

If I'm being honest, I felt betrayed. Here I had thought "alternative culture" was going to protect me from ever having to feel embarrassed, and instead it was making me feel like even more of a loser. And while I wish I could say that my discomfort with dancing led me to realize/admit that I did not believe, after all, that authentic art could only be produced by people in thrall to their unencumbered instincts, the truth is it took a few more years for that particular fever to break. The day it did—the day I realized that the imperative to only ever follow your gut and never think about anything amounted to a kind of bullying—was the day I finally became a well-adjusted, happy adult.

I should warn you before I get into it: what happened did not involve Juiceboxxx in any way, though it did involve a band he likes and is kind of friends with. That band was called Wavves, and what follows is the story of why I hate them.

2.

I saw Wavves in concert during the tail end of summer 2010, at a club in Williamsburg I had never been to before. This was back when I worked at the *New York Observer*, a small weekly paper where I covered the book publishing industry and the art world, but was more or less free to pitch stories on whatever I wanted. By this point in my life I had largely stopped paying attention to new bands—not so much because I was alienated by them, but because I had simply found other things to care about. But thanks to a new friend who blogged about music, I spent that summer feeling newly invested in it. I began buying records for the first time in years and attending lots of shows at underground spaces around Brooklyn. In particular I became somewhat fixated on a group of friends who grew up in the suburbs of New Jersey, who all played in bands together during high school, and had rather unexpectedly become successful indie rock musicians after graduating from college.

My interest in this group was personal, because one of the guys who played music with them during high school, a drummer named Peter, was a member of the band I was in during my first year of college. Peter and I were in the same freshman dorm, and in the course of getting to know one another, we played our juvenilia for each other and traded stories about the music scenes, such as they were, in our respective hometowns.

I really loved the songs Peter played me by his former band; I also really liked the wistful warmth with which he talked about the other former members, most of whom, like Peter, had gone off to liberal arts colleges around the country, like Bennington and Hampshire and the University of Wisconsin–Madison.

I remember how shocked I was when years after we became friends, Peter told me that some of the guys he used to play with had started a new band called Real Estate, and that their music was starting to get written about and championed by *Pitchfork*. Soon they were everywhere, receiving coverage in glossy magazines, playing major summer festivals, and touring the world behind a very pretty, very delicate album they had released on a well-respected record label. More than anything else, Real Estate was classic indie rock: polite, educated, and contemplative.

Peter, by that point, had happily committed to becoming an academic, and I don't really know if he felt any longing to be with his old friends as they sailed off on their rock-and-roll adventure. For me, though, it was thrilling to watch these guys become stars not only because I knew their old drummer, or because it validated my enthusiasm for their early bedroom recordings, but because they seemed like such normal, intelligent people: guys who weren't that different from me, and who I probably would have been friends with if we'd gone to the same high school or college. These were young men who would have probably gone out into the world and gotten jobs much like I was about to do, if things hadn't broken for them the way they did.

During the summer of 2010, Real Estate was peaking, as

were a bunch of other young musicians in their extended orbit who grew up either in the same New Jersey town or in the next one over. The music they made varied pretty widely, but it had in common a determined headiness. As laid back as some of it was, the bands sounded like they were trying their hardest, and were taking care to make things they were proud of.

It was in that context that Wavves appeared on my radar. Wavves did not make heady or careful music. They were sloppy and rowdy, and their songs were uniformly slathered in lots of fuzz and messy distortion. Their melodies, while catchy, were not written with the intention of sounding beautiful, while their lyrics were straightforward and never contained any words that were longer than a few syllables. They were a bratty pop punk band, basically, and they were pleased with themselves for making music that had a stupid kind of urgency to it. The lead singer of Wavves, Nathan Williams, talked in interviews about how he lived with his parents after high school and smoked weed in his room all day. He wore a baseball cap wherever he went and had a reputation for drinking too much and doing too many drugs.

That summer I attended maybe half a dozen shows featuring members of Real Estate and their affiliates, and interviewed a lot of them for what was going to be an article about their hometown. What I hoped to describe in my piece was the unlikely joy I suspected they felt at getting to be rock stars, after spending their teenage years dreaming about it but nevertheless doing pretty much everything they were supposed to do as middle class kids, whose parents cared about their grades and hoped they would go on to enjoy stable, lucrative careers.

Then I went to that Wavves concert in Williamsburg, and my plans for the story I was going to write rearranged themselves.

What happened was I got really angry—first at Nathan Williams and the two meatballs who served as his bandmates, who spent the entire set making fun of people in the crowd for being nerdy hipsters with college degrees, and then at the audience, who lapped it up as if these idiots actually were better than us, just because they were unvarnished and crude.

"Hey, if anybody's writing anything out there, I can't read," one of the Wavves guys who wasn't Williams said at one point, implicitly addressing all the rock critics in the room. "Pretty good think piece, right?" Earlier, he had said something sarcastic about Williams having been cooler when he was just a "naïve college grad," and then interrupted himself to say, "Just kidding. He didn't graduate from college. Me neither. We all quitted. 'Cause we dumb!"

Everyone laughed at this shit like it was hilarious, reminding me of that famous *Simpsons* scene where Homer is watching a black stand-up comedian on TV make fun of how white people drive, and squealing through his laughter, "It's true! We're so lame!"

I ended up writing a piece that basically said the Wavves

guys were morons, and that I didn't see what was so admirable about that, or what was so unforgivably ridiculous about being educated and caring about things and being ambitious. The Real Estate posse, who conveniently were playing a big show right around the corner the following night, served as my counterpoint: here were guys who didn't brag about being simple, who didn't take pride in being "intuitive" as opposed to considered and deliberate. The night after my story came out, Wavves played a private show in Manhattan that was attended almost exclusively by music writers and industry people, and in between songs Williams announced that if anyone wanted to write any rude blog posts about the show, they should go talk to him after his set so he could punch them in the face. Later he dedicated a song to me. "This song is called 'Fuck the *New York Observer*,'" he said, and all of my colleagues in the media cheered.

3.

All that stuff settled strangely in my head, and in the immediate aftermath I felt bitter and furious about being forced to participate in a culture that equated stupidity with sincerity and authenticity. I decided that the ideology around dancing was just one manifestation of this much broader, and profoundly toxic, worldview that said being mindless and stupid was the key to living a truly liberated life, while being thoughtful and calculated made it impossible to be true to your real self.

It's fair to wonder, in light of this, how I can tolerate, let alone love and look up to, someone like Juiceboxxx—who, as you may remember, invited me to a Wavves concert when he first arrived in New York, and considers everyone in the band his good friends. This is a guy, after all, who once wrote a song in which he said, "I don't rap 'cuz I'm smart or clever / I rap 'cuz it's in my heart forever," as if the two were mutually exclusive. This is also a guy who released a dance single, written in the second person, in which the climax has him taking your hand and walking you down the path to party-town:

First you feel the vibe,
Then you feel the love,
Then you feel the beat,
Then you move above!
Then you go insane!
Then you raise your hands!
Then you move your feet!
Then you understand!

Based on all that I should find Juiceboxxx appalling. I should want to tell him to go fuck himself and stop trying to tell people how to live their lives. I know I should. And yet I don't. Because for all my impassioned crowing about how there's nothing wrong with being a self-conscious pencil-neck who is constitutionally incapable of dancing and going out of his mind, it would appear that being under the influence of Juiceboxxx makes me wish I wasn't one of them.

This is the problem, then: As much as I despise the idea that one must be capable of having thoughtless, unhinged fun in order to be truly alive—and I do despise it a lot, maybe more than I despise anything else, to the point where I've argued, in my more extreme moods, that it amounts to a generic form of anti-Semitism—it seems that I pretty much totally buy into it when it's coming from Juice. Even if it does bother me to hear him say on a record that he doesn't "make music for nerds to do math to," I can't deny that every single time I've gone to one of his shows I have hoped my hardest, with zero resentment, that I would be able to somehow absorb his spirit and let it move me around the way I know it's meant to. When I've watched other people open themselves up like this in these situations, it has struck me as the closest thing that—to use those words I liked so much in college—mere critics like myself can do in order to achieve the state of total freedom that geniuses, like Juiceboxxx, are able to channel at will.

Thinking about this as I sit across from him at dinner at the Mexican restaurant and listen to him talk about how intuitive he is, I feel a little hollow inside. I wonder, privately, about why Juice has the effect on me that he does—why watching him play, and even just being around him, makes me want so badly to summon in myself the kind of free-wheeling abandon he raps about, or why he has the power to convince me that achieving that state actually would make me a better, more complete person. When I come up with exactly nothing, I resolve to just ask him what he thinks about it, as an artist.

3.

Before I get an opportunity to pull the trigger on this question, the conversation shifts to the upcoming November tour, and suddenly Juice is laying out for me what sounds like an extremely well-defined mission statement.

"I want the shows to have a lot of guts and a lot of tension," he says, "but I also want them to be fun, and I want them to have a certain classic sense of rock-and-roll entertainment. I'm trying to walk the line between being really raw and putting on a really great show. Because anything on either side of that fence feels safe to me."

When I ask him what he means by "safe" and what the alternative is, he explains to me that he's always wanted his performances to split the difference between extreme tension and pure fun, which has meant channeling the confrontational stance of all the noise and hardcore bands he grew up seeing at Milwaukee basement shows, while also striving for the kind of accessibility and populism that he sees reflected in the mainstream hip-hop he has always loved, and the Bruce Springsteen, James Brown, and Cheap Trick performances he watches, worshipfully, on YouTube. He's well aware, Juice says, that to date he has been much more successful at the confrontation thing than the other thing. But his new goal is to change that: the mission he feels he's on, he tells me, even as he considers completely walking away from the Juiceboxxx project, is to make himself into an act that everyone, even people who only listen to top-40 pop, can love without trying. Hopefully, he says, the upcoming tour will serve as a big step forward on this front.

"I've seen enough fucking noise bands that are like ten times wilder than me, but I don't come away from that feeling inspired, because it's kind of easy to do that," he says. "What's harder is to do that and still be making pop music."

It catches me completely off guard that he has such specific goals, given that all the times I've seen him play live, he has looked like a person having some kind of out-of-body experience that he couldn't really answer for or talk about in terms of intentionality or goals. I had always assumed that if someone asked him how he does what he does, he'd say he just goes up there and lets the spirit take him away—an assumption that I thought had been validated when I posed that very question to him just a few minutes earlier.

I ask Juice if the fact that he has all these specific aesthetic ambitions means that his stage show is a lot more consciously calibrated than I had thought. When he says yes I tell him that surprises me, because the main thing I've always felt when watching him play—the thing I've always assumed I was responding to, and what I've always told people about when trying to convince them to come see him with me—was that Juiceboxxx is an artist without self-awareness: a creature running on spinal urges and unprocessed fuel and thus achieving a kind of self-driving majesty that most people are utterly incapable of conjuring.

"Well, once you get on stage, you can have certain ideas about what you want to do, but the only way it's ever gonna be good is if you execute it with a certain level of pure, unfiltered passion," he says. "I'm in total control but I'm totally out of control at the same time, you know? It's beyond words. It's everything at once. My brain's going at a thousand miles a minute but at the same time I'm not thinking about anything.

"You can't bullshit on stage," he adds. "It doesn't lie. You have to fucking bring it. You can have all these influences, all this knowledge, but the hope is that just from giving a hundred percent, you transcend all that stuff and end up being yourself, and becoming something exciting and new."

For a moment I interpret this as him backtracking, like he's realized he's let me behind a curtain in a way that might ruin him for me. But then I realize he's actually just trying to have it both ways, and while it sounds nice—a compromise between the head and the heart—I don't totally buy it.

"See, I think most people see self-consciousness in direct opposition to authenticity," I say to him, prevailing over the queasiness I feel at having to utter such words. "I've always thought of you as sort of exemplifying that—like, being real by virtue of not being self-aware."

Even if that weren't true, I say, it's a fact that our generation has been encouraged and taught to believe that irony and sincerity are opposites, and that a person incapable of the former is the only sort you could ever truly trust. This is why it's always so electrifying, I say, for us to encounter people who seem like they "can't help but be the way they are," whose behavior and style are not matters of choice but of nature. I'm positive Juiceboxxx knows this, and I'm intent on getting him to stop pretending he doesn't.

But Juice balks. "Well, I don't think that's true at all," he says, an unfriendly edge creeping into his voice that I haven't heard before, which makes me scared that I have said something terrible. "I mean, I consider myself to be very self-conscious, in some ways. I don't know. I don't put myself in opposition to anybody else. I think everybody's just trying to be themselves, you know?"

I can tell by how vague he's getting that the conversation is making him nervous, but I'm not willing to let it drop. At this point I badly want him to acknowledge that he and I are in fact very different. And also to feel sorry for me. And also to tell me it's OK that I am who I am.

"It's easier for some people to be themselves than it is for others," I say. "Like, especially when I was younger, the couple of times you and I hung out, I worried about whether I could keep up with you. I wanted to be more of a live wire, more spontaneous, like you."

Though I sound like a child saying these things, I power through, in part because it feels good to be honest, but also because I think I am flattering him in a way that will make him soften. Instead it seems to make him only more defensive. "I don't know, man," he says. "Maybe to you at certain points I seemed like this manic rager or something, and surely I have those moments, but I also have a lot of deep-seated fucking problems with my life, you know?" He sounds for a second like he's about to be more specific, but then it's like his engine stalls. He starts about ten different sentences ("I mean, the thing is—there's all different levels of like—it's just natural—I feel like you're putting me in a—") before finally giving up.

"This is just a zone where I feel uncomfortable making statements because it feels like I'm out of my depth intellectually," he says. "I feel self-conscious right now because I feel like I don't have the depth to maybe answer these questions, or to make any sort of statements on anything besides, just, rock-and-roll music, you know? Like, I don't know, man. Juiceboxxx has just been a really weird attempt at me not killing myself for twelve years."

I experience a pang of anger that he's pulling this card— that he's saying, basically, that I'm overthinking things in a way that doesn't make sense to him because he's just such a helplessly natural person. But I can also tell that he sounds upset, and so, more than anything, I feel like I've messed up.

After dinner, as I walk down the street, alone, I try to wrap my mind around the idea of Juiceboxxx as a meticulous and deliberate thinker—an artist with a vision for what he wants to be that did not come fully formed, but has been carefully refined, by him, through hard work and self-reflection. I wonder if by worshipping him as an unthinking "genius," I've been denying him credit that he would say he deserves, and I feel briefly ashamed as it occurs to me, for the first time ever, that he might not like being thought of as a wild animal.

For so long I had believed that true artistic greatness meant not knowing what was good about what you were doing. But maybe I was wrong about this, and as I turn the possibility over in my head, I find I am profoundly relieved. Maybe I don't need to feel like a hypocrite for loving Juiceboxxx, after all. And maybe, just maybe, that means the difference between people like him and people like me is less black and white than I have always assumed.

5

NEON HUNK, ETC.

I.

I'm on a Greyhound bus, headed to Boston for work, when I decide to avail myself of the on-board wireless in order to go through the entirety of Juiceboxxx's blog, which I've read only sporadically up to this point. My plan, directly inspired by my happy, newfound confusion about what makes Juiceboxxx Juiceboxxx, is to read the blog from the beginning, in chronological order, while listening to his complete discography start to finish on my headphones. To be honest, it feels more like repentance for past sins than research—an attempt to understand Juice's mind after years of buying into the "pure id" bullshit that I'm now convinced is only one layer of his artistry.

What I'm overwhelmed by first as I start reading is the sheer volume of what Juice knows about music. While there are many loving references to genuinely mainstream music—in 2011, I discover, he posted an incredible DJ mix featuring the likes of Bob Seger, Aaliyah, Wyclef Jean, and Bruce Springsteen—he writes with familiarity about bands and record labels I've never heard of, regional dance styles I didn't know existed, and obscure radio DJs from the '80s and '90s whom he seems to truly admire and regard as important figures in the history of pop culture.

For the most part the individual blog posts he writes about this stuff take the form of passionate endorsements, and the overall tone is humble, reverential, and at times borderline delusional in terms of how "legendary" he thinks some DIY venue or experimental noise band was or deserves to be.

In one post he links to an archive of music put out by a label called Hanson Records, which I gather was founded by members of an unusually successful noise band called Wolf Eyes that I've actually heard of. "CRUCIAL PIECE OF HEARTLAND FREAKOUT HISTORY RIGHT HERE, PEOPLE!" Juice writes, by way of explaining a washed-out YouTube video he has posted that is twenty-two minutes long and consists of two guys screaming and making horrible atonal sounds with their guitars. To my eyes and ears, it is completely unwatchable and unlistenable. If this weren't the case, perhaps I would be as excited as Juice evidently was to discover that "THE LABEL'S VIMEO PAGE IS FULL OF SICK ARCHIVAL FOOTAGE!"

Noise music was Juice's first love, something I found out

when I drove up to Milwaukee the summer after high school ended to see him play, and had to walk out of the basement where the show was taking place because the opening act just sounded like soul-destroying screeching to me. Sitting here on the bus a decade later, as I try to get through this Hanson Records video he's so excited about, I wonder for the hundredth time in my life what exactly is wrong with me that I don't like noise music at all—that I can't even identify with anyone who does, or understand what it does for them.

The other stuff Juice really enjoys makes just as little sense to me. In one blog post he talks about something called *Massive Magazine*, which I guess was a zine about rave music based out of Milwaukee. As a twelve-year-old kid, Juice writes, he was lucky enough to "catch the tail end" of the publication's existence, "just as rave culture was start-ing to decline in Wisconsin." This alone amazes me, as it implies that Juiceboxxx could also say when rave culture peaked in Wisconsin, and what it was like when it did. He could also probably explain why it went into decline, and what's been up with it since. Personally I can't fathom be-ing this interested in or knowledgeable about rave culture; in fact I can't even listen to rave music for more than sixty seconds, assuming I'm even correct about what rave music is. But my respect for Juice's enthusiasm and expertise is intense, and I ask myself if there's anything on earth I know as much about.

What really gets me are all the entries where he ecstat-ically describes finding online databases of downloadable

DJ mixes and other ephemera that originally aired on radio and TV decades ago. In one post he links to a YouTube page with a collection of old public access dance shows from Detroit which he calls "very important documentation of pure American energy," and says it has almost moved him to tears "on many occasions." Elsewhere he links to a cache of radio mixes that "span the entire history of house music." "It is so easy to get lost in here," he writes, referencing DJs with names like Farley Jackmaster Funk and Bad Boy Bill.

Needless to say I have no idea what he's talking about with any of this stuff, and it boggles my mind that he can write about it with this level of detail. And while my admiration doesn't translate into any kind of desire to force myself into liking stuff I just don't like, it does confirm for me that, as untethered as Juiceboxxx might appear on stage, the reality is that he is a deeply obsessive music fan with copious, elaborate, and above all, idiosyncratic inputs that he takes very seriously.

As far as I'm concerned, this is pretty much the definition of having taste. And to be clear, when I say "taste" I'm not talking about refinement but sensibility: a singular and consistent mechanism that draws you to certain things in the world and motivates you to seek them out. Most of us don't have such a mechanism; instead, we have preferences, meaning we stick our heads out of our holes every once in a while, inhale whatever books, movies, music, and TV shows are in the air as they fly past us in the form of Twitter links and magazine articles, and then decide what of it we like and what we like less. This is why, ultimately, even those of us who self-identify as being well-informed and engaged in culture end up being into more or less the same stuff as all our friends and acquaintances.

Then there are people like Juiceboxxx, whose sensibility is so particular and so self-directed that it makes him different from everybody else on the planet. And while I've always known about his attraction to musical subcultures and avant-garde art, I've never before appreciated how systematically he took it all in. Because it's not like there's no one else out there who loves '80s and '90s house music. I'm sure there are lots of people who do. But as I go through Juice's blog, I keep thinking about how direct the line is between what he's put into his head, and what comes out of him when he's on stage. It's impressive to me that his aesthetic universe is so full of stuff that he himself decided, consciously, to populate it with—pieces of culture he meticulously picked out, from all the culture that exists in the world, and made into part of who he is.

I compare this in my mind to someone like me, who not always but sometimes solves the problem of choosing what music to listen to by putting iTunes on fucking shuffle.

2.

When I return to New York, it's already October 21, which means Juiceboxxx will be leaving for the Thunder Zone tour in something like ten days. He's been going out on the town a lot, going to dance parties and clubs with Dre Skull and other old friends, and rehearsing with his new drummer at a practice space in Bushwick. In about a week Willy will be flying in from Milwaukee so the three of them can hammer out their set.

Juice and I have plans tonight to hang out in Williamsburg; I've insisted on going to see where he has been staying, because I'm curious to see what his room looks like and also because he mentioned he could play me a few songs that will appear on his new EP. On the walk to the subway I listen to a song called "Never Surrender Forever," which I've been playing for everyone I've told about Juiceboxxx over the past couple of weeks because it's one of the very few songs in his catalog—maybe the only one, actually—that someone who isn't already rooting for him can be expected to like immediately.

What's special about this song, which first appeared in the form of a demo on the *Thunder Zone Volume 1* mixtape from 2010 and then again as the last track of *I Don't Wanna Go into the Darkness*, is that it contains absolutely no rapping. Instead it's basically just an indie pop song, built around a pretty, wistful chord progression and a touching, intimate vocal melody. The lyrics are all about chasing the best possible version of yourself and not giving up, but Juice sounds so tired and so beaten down and so alone as he sings them that by the time the second chorus arrives, all you can think about is, "How long can he possibly keep this up?" Written in the second person, the "you" in the song is clearly Juice, which is to say it's transparently a pep talk to himself.

> *Ain't nobody gonna keep it alive*
> *but you've got that dream inside.*
> *Living in a town that don't even care*
> *So you go for a ride.*
> *And for just a little while everything's all right*
> *Searching for a dream that lives in the night*
> *Never surrender forever, never surrender forever, never*
>   *surrender forever.*

Maybe that reads as trite on paper. I don't know. All I can say is that walking down the street with it in my head, hearing him sing these words in a tone of voice that suggests a truly precarious footing on the border between despair and hope, I imagine Juice recording this in a studio and it actually puts a lump in my throat.

I think about how pretty much everyone who hears this song recognizes its beauty, and how ever since it came out, I've put it on countless times for friends of mine while driving them home late at night. Usually people just go still as it plays, the layers of dread and optimism contained in Juice's uneasy singing voice washing over them, and making them want to know him in a way nothing else in his catalog ever seems to.

3.

As I approach the address Juice has given me, I realize that
I am around the corner from an apartment I used to live in
a few years ago with a graphic designer named Guillermo
who moonlighted as a photographer, and a fashion designer
named Paola who had just moved from Mexico to try and
make it in New York. The fact that I can almost see this old
apartment from Juice's door gives me a little thrill for some
reason—I guess because I usually feel like he and I exist in
such different universes, and this is very literal evidence to
the contrary.

"So did you find this place on Craigslist?" I ask, after he
walks me upstairs through a cavernous but handsomely
lit living room. No, he says, it belongs to his friend Jacob,
who plays in that band Extreme Animals that's going on
the Thunder Zone tour, and who was part of Paper Rad, the
art collective that Juice got connected with when he was in
high school. Jacob is out of town, which is why Juice is able
to stay here, but it remains to be seen, he says, what's going
to happen once Jacob comes back in a few days.

We walk past someone who looks like he's studying for
a test as we make our way up a set of stairs, and when I
ask Juice in a quiet voice if the person is his roommate, he
says yes but that he doesn't really know him. Upon entering
his tiny, closet-like lair, Juice sits down on the edge of the
bed and I shift my weight from one leg to the other before
finally perching on the edge of a dresser. There's a pair of
boxers emblazoned with little *Dark Side of the Moon* prisms

hanging from a hook beside the bed. When I ask Juice if they are his, the answer is "No, they're Jacob's." I imagine what it must be like to live in a place where someone else's underwear is dangling above you while you sleep and you don't even care enough to move them.

The room is dark and smells like a sleeping person; there are records and DVDs everywhere, and a suitcase flung open on the floor that's piled high with clothes. I ask Juice if it's all he brought to New York with him and he says yes, except that there's new stuff coming in the mail for him every day related to the tour, including a huge vinyl banner someone made for him that says WELCOME TO THE THUNDER ZONE that's going to be pinned above the stage at every venue he plays. "I've just been getting all these packages," he says, in reference to all the merch he's going to be selling—not only T-shirts, CDs, and records, but also the energy drink he created, and a VHS tape of experimental videos by Jacob's band. All this stuff has been trickling in via UPS over the past few days, Juice says, which has been especially stressful because he accidentally gave some of the vendors the wrong address.

Juice is wearing a hoodie and a jacket with the NBC logo on the back; his skin looks a lot clearer than the last time I saw him, and compared to our most recent conversation he seems totally relaxed and on point. Something about seeing him in this context, living with other people in a Williamsburg apartment, makes me imagine seeing him in the street and not knowing who he is. I realize that, not unlike my mom, I'd probably dismiss him as a typical hipster dressed in thrift store scraps. When Juice asks if I want to hear some of the new songs, it makes me wonder how many of the people I write off in this way go home to a room where they make things they've devoted their lives to.

4.

He opens his laptop up on the bed and puts on an as-yet-unreleased music video for a song called "Front Seat," which he filmed while in the Midwest shortly before coming to New York, on a beach alongside Lake Michigan.

As the video starts I see that Juice looks objectively glamorous in it, standing against a beautiful rising sun, and wearing black jeans and an unzipped denim jacket exposing his bare chest. In the moments before the beat kicks in, he wades into the water with his shoes on. Then, as the song really gets going, he's standing on the beach and looking out toward the horizon, keeping time with his hand against his outer thigh.

"Front Seat" announces itself as a true rap-rock song right away, with a heavy metal guitar riff and big 4/4 drums. As Juice starts rapping, my main reaction is that he sounds more confident in his style than I've ever seen or heard him—unapologetic, revved up, certain that the song is sounding out loud the way it did in his head when he wrote it. I try to listen for the words, and though I only pick out a few lines here and there over the running commentary Juice is providing about the filming of the video, what I do hear is personal and funny and specific. At one point the guitar falls out and Juice raps, in a tone of voice that sounds more adult and more conversational than he's ever sounded on a recording, "I don't know why I haven't given up yet / I don't know why I don't give a fuck yet / nothing in my life is a fucking safe bet / Can't stop, but I probably won't make it!!!"

I punctuate that last bit with three exclamation points because that's how he sounds when he delivers the line—sure-footed, defiant, unafraid. The song ends less than a minute later and I'm beyond thrilled with it. The video, in my opinion, most of which Juiceboxxx spends with his hair wet and his shirt wide open, makes him look extremely cool.

"That was really good," I say, unsure if the point of him showing it to me was to get my feedback or what. Regardless, he doesn't react to the praise at all, his eyes stuck on the computer screen, where he's clicking around in what looks like a piece of recording software and queuing up something else. He then plays me eight versions of a Target jingle he recorded the night before—tryouts for an ad the company is trying to put on the air in time for Thanksgiving.

5.

After the jingles finish I look around the room and see posters for Extreme Animals, and by way of making small talk while Juice continues fiddling with his laptop I ask what kind of music they play. Juice acts surprised that I've never heard them before and explains that they make a hybrid of noisy electronic music and video collage. He pulls up one of their videos on YouTube to show me, and what I see after he hits play doesn't make sense to me at all. I won't even try to describe it, but I guess what you'd call it is video collage, played over a crunchy interpolation of the theme from Harry Potter, and cut with all kinds of seemingly random, vaguely creepy clips. There are women dancing in a circle, there is a guy holding a cat with a crucifix around its neck, there are flashes of text that say things like "WHO AM I?" and "I AM YOU" that don't seem to correspond with anything. I watch silently, baffled at the thought of someone sitting down and putting these things together and arranging them in a specific order, somehow making decisions about what goes where. It feels utterly arbitrary to me, and meaningless.

After it's over Juiceboxxx luckily doesn't wait for my reaction before asking if I want to hear one more song off his EP before we go grab something to eat. Relieved, I say yes with excitement that turns into real, anticipatory elation when he says off-handedly that it's a straightforward rock song that's going to remind me of "Never Surrender Forever." The name of the song is "Open Up Your Life," and I'll describe it later; suffice it to say, for now, that on first listen it strikes me as an undeniable pop hit that everyone, not just me, will love. When Juice tells me afterwards that he's trying to write more songs like this, I can't help but wonder what would happen if rapping simply and naturally fell out of his repertoire, and whether there's any possible future in which he just writes these gorgeous melodies, and doesn't insist on pursuing the aspects of his sound that have made him so unpalatable to so many people for so many years.

As we're putting on our coats he mentions that he might fly out to the Bay Area soon and film a video for one of the songs off the EP because his friend has agreed to do it for one hundred dollars. "He was in this band called Neon Hunk," he says. "I don't know if you remember them. They were really seminal around a certain era."

6.

For dinner we go to a restaurant a few blocks from Juice's apartment called Grand Morelos. It's a place I was introduced to by my friend Nick, who worked as a music journalist for about five years after college, before starting a band, learning how to produce and record, and ultimately devoting himself entirely to playing music and running a record label. I mention this only because Nick is the only guy I know who started out as what I would have called a "secondary source"—a critic, basically—and made himself a primary one through sheer force of will and talent. The fact that he did it in his late twenties has always made me wonder if I've been wrong to assume that people are inevitably too far gone by that point to make the transition.

After we settle in I confess to Juiceboxxx that I had no idea what was going on in that Extreme Animals video he showed me in his room. I also admit that I have never been able to enjoy noise music of any kind, and that I had never heard of Neon Hunk in my life.

"Yeah," Juice says, in a tone of voice that indicates he already knows this about me. "Well, it's because you were doing things like going to college and getting a job. You have to understand, sometimes when I talk about this stuff, I'm not—I feel embarrassed, almost, that I have this knowledge—"

"No, I feel embarrassed—" I say, cutting him off before getting cut off right back.

"Well maybe we both . . ." he starts, but to my great chagrin doesn't finish his sentence. "Look, you have to understand that, if you think you feel embarrassed, I feel embarrassed that this is what I've spent my life doing. In a way, it's really bleak. Like when you're so deep in the vortex of a certain kind of niche culture, it's easy to take it as your reality. But when you step outside of it, it can just look so dumb, you know?"

A lot of times, Juice says, noise shows with a bunch of bands on the bill end up being de facto competitions for who can be the most alienating, the most out-there: the noise Olympics, he calls them. "That's why pop music has always appealed to me," he says. "It transcends some super-petty things that often exist in niche cultures."

Personally, I've always been drawn to niche cultures, even if I never actually immersed myself in any of them. One of my favorite stories I've written in recent years, for example, was about a community of young people who design board games, and have all kinds of terminology and specialized concepts they use to discuss how to make a game fun. I can remember being attracted to groups like this, being curious about their rules and values, when I was a kid too, and feeling a desire to embed myself in them. In fifth grade I would covetously watch groups of skateboarders hang out by my school; in college, I became fascinated by the world of policy debate and wrote an article about all their strange rituals and traditions.

For better or for worse, the only time I've ever really tried to join a subculture was in middle school, when I tried to find my footing in the world of ska-punk music. During this period I expended great energy and money on ordering CDs from ska-punk mail-order catalogs, buying T-shirts after ska-punk concerts that would identify me as a fan of ska-punk to the outside world, and thinking very hard in the privacy of my bedroom about things like, "Does No Doubt count as ska-punk?"

A similar thing happened to Juiceboxxx when he was a kid, I think, except he glommed onto a whole array of subcultures at once—not just noise and punk, but also all the regional dance scenes that he rhapsodizes about on his blog—instead of trying to build his whole identity around one in particular. His problem now, he tells me between bites of a sandwich, is that all his friends still come from those scenes, but more and more he's been feeling like he has to extricate himself from all of them if he ever wants to achieve real success.

"There are certain things I continue to go back to, that have probably been messing with my true aspirations," he says, sounding frustrated with himself. "At a certain point I probably should have been like, 'OK, I shouldn't be touring with noise bands and punk bands anymore.' But I've always tried to have it both ways."

By that he means he's been working to make his output more and more broadly appealing, while maintaining a reputation among fans of weirdo marginal music as a performer who can push boundaries and make audiences uncomfortable in the way all those people aspire to. More than that, he says, it's just something that's inside of him—that impulse for confrontation he told me about earlier, which he got from watching bands in basements during his adolescence, and which has carried over into his often-tumultuous, borderline violent live shows. For much of his career, that impulse has been locked in combat with Juice's desire to belt out a positive, friendly message, and if I had to boil down Juice's work to its essence, I'd point to the particular way in which those two things mix together. It's a dynamic you can hear all over *I Don't Wanna Go into the Darkness*—you can even see it on the cover, which shows a silhouette of Juiceboxxx standing on a mountaintop, with a dark city behind him, against a sun that's either rising or setting.

"Sometimes you get beat by the night, you're living on

NEON HUNK, ETC.   117

the edge but you feel all right," he raps on "21 on the 101," the album's centerpiece. "You're on the road / you look to the sky / you're on a mission but you don't know why."

7.

"My whole thing is that I've always wanted to insert myself into these different contexts, but do the same performance— so, not tone down the aggressiveness for the dance clubs, but also not tone down the poppiness in the punk clubs," Juice says after ordering coffee. "And that's always put me in sort of a gray zone."

Listening to Juice talk about noise and punk music, and giving voice to the idea that his allegiance to those scenes has held him back, I feel somewhat absolved of blame for having been such a failure as his evangelist. The problem, I realize, is that even though Juice's music is in certain ways super straightforward, and even though I'm not used to thinking of rap as anything other than a type of pop, the fact of the matter is that he has actively worked against being easy to like because all the people he's friends with, all the musicians he sees as peers, operate on the belief that being hard to like is a virtue. I wonder what might happen now that he seems on the cusp of finally cutting ties with that way of looking at things, and dedicating himself entirely to making music that ordinary people don't have to strain to enjoy.

"I'm very aware that I'm still getting better," he says,

when I tell him how impressed I was with the stuff he played me in his apartment. "And, you know, that's what's so crazy about music, is that being twenty-seven puts you in a weird zone—like, you're not young anymore. But in so many other creative disciplines, I would just be starting out. If some kid started painting at fifteen and didn't become a famous painter until he was thirty-five, no one would really bat an eye. I think that's semi-common in other creative disciplines—to really put in your time and really learn what the fuck you're doing."

Then, as if embarrassed to be talking like this, he switches to a jokey voice he likes to use that makes him sound like a sleazy old guy who's being a ham: "What can I say, man? I'm a student of the game."

On the walk home I plug my headphones into my tape recorder and listen to a very low quality recording of "Open Up Your Life" that I made surreptitiously while Juice was playing it for me in his room. Even in this form, I can hear its majesty and its quiet resolve.

And when they kick you down
You've gotta open up your life
And when they knock you around
You've gotta open up your life
And when they tell you you're done
You've gotta open up your life
Oh, but man, you've just begun
You've gotta open up your life.

It sounds like something Jonathan Richman of the Modern Lovers might have written on a lonely night, I think to myself—optimistic and shot through with life-affirming guitar riffs engineered to make people feel good. It is a truly convincing song, and the best thing he's ever done by far.

6

YOU ARE INVITED

1.

The day after our evening in Williamsburg, I text Juice to say that if he needs a place to stay after his sublet runs out, he should let me know, because although our apartment isn't too big we do have a very luxurious blow-up mattress he could sleep on. I don't ask Alice about this before doing it even though I know I probably should, but I figure if he takes me up on it, I can cross that bridge when I get to it.

He doesn't respond until the next day at around five p.m.: "really appreciate that, i'll let you know," he writes. Then: "djing a house party tonight fyi."

I get these messages just as Alice and I are walking out of a movie theater in Brooklyn. It's a Friday night at the end of what has been a difficult week at work, and the excitement I feel about the prospect of going to a house party with Juiceboxxx collides with my desire to go home and fall asleep. As Alice and I walk, I tell her that Juice just texted me and that now there's this thing on the table that I'm kind of tempted to go to.

"Where is it?" she asks, and I have to admit that I don't know, and that frankly I'm not sure I have it in me to go regardless.

Nevertheless I text Juice for the address, which turns out to be right off the L train and very close to where I used to live. This makes the prospect of going somehow less unfathomable to me, so I ask Juice what time he is starting his DJ set and when he expects to be done. I realize as I send him these texts that I am asking the ultimate loser questions, and his answer makes it clear that he is not really in a position to help me: "im in deep east ny right now at this gallery for jacob's sisters opening." Well, OK, I think to myself, and all of a sudden the feeling of being on the outside of Juice's world comes rushing back to me, after having subsided to an extent as a result of the past few weeks. Once again he is riding in the distance somewhere, in a place that I do not have the keys to and where it would never occur to me to go. East New York! I know that's in Brooklyn somewhere but nothing else. That there are art galleries there certainly has never been on my radar.

I text a few people about coming with me but no one responds except my friend Fran, who is a couple of years younger than me and, perhaps relatedly, tends to be more game for spontaneous meeting up than the other people in my immediate orbit. Fran says that a random house party sounds like exactly what she's after tonight and promises to meet me there. After Alice gets in bed and I kiss her good-night, I step into the night, hoping against hope that Juice is already at the party when I arrive and that Fran doesn't take too long getting there.

2.

I text Juice when I get above ground and he replies hastily, "i think the door should be open im djing now its just getting started tho band about to play." I start to wonder about what exactly I'm walking into, and whether Juice's text message means I'm going to miss his DJ set. I'm also worried because I promised Fran there would be dancing at this party, but knowing the company Juiceboxxx keeps there is a signifi-cant chance that the band in question will be a noise band.

As these thoughts run through my head I look and look but I can't find the place. Reluctantly, I text Juice and admit that I'm lost. He responds right away, and steers me toward a white locked gate that I somehow missed.

When I walk in, looking around for familiar faces and not seeing any, I stash my coat in a corner, and notice there is no furniture anywhere except a table in the middle of the room with bottles of liquor on it. It takes me a few minutes to realize that everyone around me is between eight and ten years younger than me; I briefly consider writing down in the little notebook I've brought with me descriptions of what everyone looks like, but I decide I lack the vocabulary and shouldn't bother. Suffice it to say that there are people here with all kinds of strange haircuts.

I don't see Juiceboxxx anywhere so I pour myself a plastic cup of Jim Beam, no ice because there is none, and start poking around the house in search of him. After two laps through the living room and out onto the back porch, where there are about fifty kids huddled together smoking, I finally realize there is a basement, with the low hum of music rising from it. There, I find Juice hunched over his laptop, playing something I don't recognize but that he tells me later is a 1989 song called "Work That Mutha Fucker" by someone named Steve Poindexter.

Juice is wearing a denim hoodie with a baseball cap. I yell into his ear, "Thanks for inviting me!" and ask if it's cool that a friend of mine might be coming through in a little while. Juice smiles in a friendly way at this, and gestures toward our surroundings as if to emphasize how unlikely it is that anyone in this chaotic environment would ever notice or care that a stranger had entered their midst. When I ask him if I've missed the majority of his set he shakes his head and says he'll be DJing all night once the band is done.

Conscious of the fact that he's busy, I say I'm going to let him get back to DJing and that we can catch up after he's done. I text Fran to see what time she's coming, and wander around the party some more before grabbing a Bud Light from a mostly full carton that's sitting on top of an amplifier. I find a spot to stand while Juice DJs and the band that's about to play sets up their instruments. After a minute I notice a big guy to my left glancing suspiciously in my direction. He and the girl he's talking to are both drinking Bud Light, so I'm pretty sure I know what's going on, but I don't let on that I've done anything wrong and keep sipping and bobbing my head to Juice's music. After a minute the big guy goes over to the carton of Bud Light and picks it up, and when he walks back to where he was standing, he doesn't put it back down again. I take this to mean he does not want me to take any more of his beer, and I'm reminded of a traumatic event that took place one summer at camp, when I stole an Airhead from some kid's bedroom—I had never had one before and wanted to try it—and got caught. This situation with the Bud Light, I think to myself, is not nearly as bad, but even so, when you're alone at a party with a bunch of strangers who all know each other and something like that happens, it doesn't really roll off your back.

I finish the beer as quickly as I can, and as I do, Juice tucks his laptop under his shoulder and the band starts playing. I'm surprised to realize that a sizable group of people has descended into the basement to listen to them.

The band sounds like they'd fit right in on the side stage at the Warped Tour: very dramatic and abstract lyrics about the vocalist's stormy inner life, pithy choruses, riffs that want to be catchy but are actually just generic. As they play through their first song, more of their fans come downstairs, until finally we are packed in shoulder to shoulder. As the second song starts, people start pushing each other, head banging, and so on, forcing me against the back wall, where I can avoid getting shoved. I haven't been to a concert with moshing since I was a teenager, and though I am bigger and more solid now I feel about as vulnerable to injury as I did then.

Without really meaning to, I imagine dying down here with these people as I look at the ceiling above my head and the two concrete columns holding it up. It seems not so farfetched that something awful could happen, and it strikes me as urgent that I leave immediately and go upstairs.

After making my way out of the "pit" I wander aimlessly out to the back porch, where I spot Juiceboxxx talking to someone I don't know, and holding the laptop he's been DJing with high above his head in an attempt to keep it above the scrum of bodies that is squeezing by him. I nervously sidle up, worried that I'm interrupting, but Juice quickly introduces me to his friend, who turns out to be Jacob, the guy with the Pink Floyd boxers who rented Juiceboxxx his room. Jacob is short and gentle-looking, with a normal haircut, a normal T-shirt, and wireframe glasses— not at all what I imagined Juice's cool friend who founded an art collective would look like.

Yelling into my ear so that I can hear him over the noise, Juice says he has to get up early the next day to record a jingle for Exxon, which he says he's feeling pretty anxious about because he's not sure if doing so will make him a major sellout. He justifies it—half-jokingly—by saying that since oil companies and corporations in general control the government, writing jingles for them and taking their checks is not that different from taking public grants, which lots of arts organizations do. "I don't know though," he says. I don't either, to be honest.

Just then some girl stumbles by and makes fun of Juice for bringing his computer to a party, and my instinct, which I thankfully suppress, is to say something in the key of, "Do you even know who you're talking to?"

After a little more small talk I go inside and stand in line for the bathroom for about ten minutes, and when I come back out to the porch I don't see Juice anywhere.

3.

After what feels like an eternity of looking around, I lean against a wall and wait for someone near me to start smoking so I can ask them for a cigarette. I wonder if I should just call it a night, since it's already after midnight, and even if Fran does show up I'm probably going to be too tired to stay out late enough to make it worth her while. But then my phone buzzes with a text from Juice, which just says, "in the yard."

I smile to myself and push my way past the porch, where I find Juice and Jacob, as well as a girl I haven't seen before, with dreadlocks and an army surplus jacket, all lounging on a hammock tied up between two trees. They're sharing a plastic water bottle full of tequila and having a conversation

with each other at an indoor volume because the party's far
enough away that they don't need to shout.

The girl, who introduces herself as Kareema, offers me
some tequila, which I gratefully drink a whole lot of in one
big gulp. I ask her, Juice, and Jacob if they know most of the
kids at this house and Juice laughs like he did before, and
they all kind of shake their heads. The reason he's here, Juice
explains, is that one of the guys who lives in the house is the
drummer who's going to be playing with him and Willy on
the Thunder Zone tour. It turns out the party is really heavy
on "the New Haven scene," which, as I find out the hard
way, does not refer to people who went to Yale, but rather
hardcore kids who hung out in basements together in the
city of New Haven, and have since moved to NYC, where
they live together in punk houses like this one and put
on shows.

As we sit and talk on the hammock, where Jacob, Kareema, and Juiceboxxx have made room for me to perch
with about half my butt, I wonder if it's my imagination that
the three of them also feel out of place here.

4.

Soon it's time for Juice to DJ again, and as we make our way
toward the house, I decide to ask him, for the first time, for
some advice with my dancing problem.

"It's not that I don't have fun when I dance at a party or
whatever, but it's very hard for me to, like, start doing it," I

say, deliberately soft-pedaling the depth of my struggle as we walk across the lawn.

I can tell that he's trying to make me feel better when he tells me that getting people to dance is mostly incumbent on the DJ. "There's a sort of science to it," he says. "A lot of it is just having the dance floor reach a certain critical mass." Someone on Twitter, he remembers, said recently that a great DJ "keeps the girls dancing and the nerds Shazam-ing," a reference to the iPhone app that can decode what song is playing if you hold it up to a speaker—the point being that the perfect DJ mix is populist but also idiosyncratic. "I've definitely Shazam-ed shit at a club before," Juice says.

"I guess for me the problem is that, like, right now, when I'm not dancing, it's completely impossible for me to imagine myself starting to dance," I say. "It feels totally unfathomable."

Juice laughs and says drinking helps. "But, I dunno, man, maybe you're just not—I dunno. I mean, I'm not the kind of guy who just turns it on and goes to the club and starts freaking out either. Nobody's really like that, I don't think."

As I let this wash over me, I get a buzz in my pocket from Fran, who has just arrived with two mutual friends of ours. After greeting them at the front door, I feel a second wind coming on despite the late hour, and we all go downstairs, expecting to join the sea of bodies grooving to whatever Juice has put on.

What we find instead is a room that's been largely de-serted since the band finished playing, except for a few scattered people along the walls and a guy who is asking a visibly unhappy Juiceboxxx if he can play along to his set on the drum kit that's been left in the middle of the room. I feel like running upstairs and telling everyone in the house that the party has finally started, that Juiceboxxx has begun his DJ set, but I know it's not my place, so I stay put.

Thanks to Fran's initiative, she and I and the other two guys who came with her start dancing, which makes me feel relieved because it means Juice has someone to play for, but also deeply uncomfortable because even when I close my eyes I don't feel drunk enough or sufficiently surrounded by people to move the way I know I ought to. As we dance in a cluster I kind of swivel my hips around and jump up and down, and at one point even twirl Fran in a circle with my index finger. There are moments when I think, "OK, I'm doing it," but mainly I feel like I've taken a drug that isn't working. Finally Fran and I decide to go get tacos around the corner; when we come back it's three in the morning and the party has ended, and we are told by someone on the back porch, where there are still a few stragglers standing around and smoking, that Juiceboxxx has gone home.

7

THE NEXT NEXT LEVEL

1.

A few days after the party, I ask Willy in an e-mail what day he's coming to New York to start rehearsals for the tour. He tells me that he's arriving the following night, October 28. From there he and Juice and the drummer will have three days to practice before renting the van and heading up to Ithaca with the rest of their tour-mates. I tell Willy I'm planning to ask Juice about maybe dropping in on one of the practice sessions in order to observe and take notes, and we discuss the possibility of making dinner plans to catch up.

I'm really excited to see Willy—the last time I got to was about three years ago—and I'm especially looking forward to hanging out with him and Juice together for the first time in my adult life. That said, I'm nervous on the day of my visit—preoccupied with the weirdness of my being there more or less in the capacity of a reporter. I'm also not certain, based on the terse way in which Juice responded when I e-mailed him to ask if I could sit in, that my presence is actually wanted. For all I know practice is a private sort of thing, a safe space where the band can talk amongst themselves and make mistakes without any kind of audience sitting there and judging them. Having a guy with a notepad in the corner is pretty much the opposite of that, obviously, but I assure myself that Juice takes this stuff seriously enough that he wouldn't have agreed to have me there if he didn't mean it.

But there's another problem, too, which is that I have a bitter, highly relevant memory lodged in my head from when I was in eighth grade, the year after Section 69 broke up, and Nigel, my bass player, joined a different band. The drummer in that band was a really popular kid at our school, whose association with the prettiest girls in our class—one of whom he dated—once landed the band a gig at a birthday party that I wasn't even close to being invited to.

I can't remember anymore how it came to be that I was in the garage with Nigel and his new band while they rehearsed during the hour or two before the party—maybe Nigel and I, who were still friends despite his decision to quit my band, had been hanging out earlier in the day—but there I was, sitting on a milk crate and listening to them run through the set of Nirvana covers they were planning to perform. I don't think my purpose was to give the band advice or weigh in with notes, but I definitely did anyway, telling them at one point that they were playing "Molly's Lips" too slow and that Jonny, the lead singer, should put more growl into the final verse of "Lounge Act."

Eventually practice ended and it came time to load up the band's gear into the back of the station wagon that Nigel's dad had brought around to the alley. I helped carry stuff while the band talked about the logistics of their arrival at the party. For whatever reason, I guess because carrying their equipment made me feel like I was part of the team, I volunteered to participate in this discussion, weighing in on when "we" were expected to get there, how long "we" would have to play, whether "we" were running late, etc. I don't know what I was counting on exactly—that by doing this I would automatically get a seat in the car and therefore get to go to the party?—but at a certain point Nigel interrupted me and reminded me that in fact there was no "we," that I was not in this band, and that there was not going to be room in the car for me given that it was already full of drums, amplifiers, and guitars. I played it off like tagging along had been the furthest thing from my mind, that I was just helping, but I never forgot it.

2.

They've already put in one full day of rehearsal and are in the middle of their second when I text Willy and Juice to say I'll probably come around eight p.m., if that's OK with them. Willy texts back to say I should call his phone when I get out of the subway and that someone will come out and grab me.

As I make my way over, I am thinking about the potential ramifications of asking Juice if I can come to Ithaca with them so that I can see the first show of the tour. I realize that in reality this is a dumb idea, since they're coming back to Brooklyn four nights later to play in Bushwick before continuing on toward Baltimore, but my reportorial instinct tells me I would gain something from seeing Juice's vision for this tour realized for the very first time. To be honest, my reportorial instinct is that I should go on the entire tour, the way William Miller does in "Almost Famous," but I know that's not going to happen, since there's no way I can take that much time off work. Going up to Ithaca seems like a good compromise, and I even consider proposing to Alice that we rent a car, book a bed and breakfast upstate where we can go the day after the show, and make a weekend of it.

What I actually want to do, though, is drive with Juice and company in the van, stop for food with them, unload with them, and go with them to whatever after-party they get taken to. When I picture this I think of a few photos that Willy sent me from one of the first tours Doom Buggy did with Juiceboxxx, in which they're getting snacks at a gas station and hanging out at a rest stop during a bathroom break. There's one, I remember, where Juiceboxxx is biting a piece of jerky, and another with Tony, the drummer, sitting on the hood of the car waiting for everyone else to pile back in. The photos were all really sunny and colorful; Willy was wearing his red hat, a blue hoodie, and drinking a twenty-ounce bottle of some soda he had just bought. There was something languid and relaxed about all of them, but also purposeful: they were driving to work, wherever work was that night.

I don't know if that's what the Thunder Zone tour is going to be like. Probably not. Probably, like any road trip, driving four hours to Ithaca is going to be a lot less fun than it sounds in principle. But I can't help wanting to come, and resolve to feel out the dynamic once I arrive at the practice space before deciding whether or not to broach the subject.

3.

By the time I arrive at the practice space they're all already outside waiting for me. They seem in good spirits; Willy has on a hoodie and a non-red knit cap covering everything but a shock of gray hair that's peeking out the front. "You're an old man now," I say, gesturing toward it and then pointing to my own speckled sideburns so as to make clear I'm not just being a jerk. "You like yours? I like mine a lot," I say. Willy smiles and makes a joke about looking distinguished that I can't make out but that I don't want to ask him to repeat. I am introduced to Mike, the drummer, who looks about five years younger than the rest of us and is wearing a black T-shirt with the sleeves ripped off.

Juiceboxxx announces that the band is about to go out and get energy drinks; I accompany them but only get a grapefruit soda. I pay last and they're already out front when I get done putting my change away. As soon as I step through the door we start crossing the street and I ask them what kind of place this is, anyway. Mike the drummer says something about how a band he's friends with usually practices there, but I'm not listening carefully enough because I'm looking at Willy and marveling at how similar he looks to the way I remember him from summer camp. There was a moment a couple of years back when he got really fat, and I'm glad to see that he's now back to normal, and that he still has the easy but shy smile of someone who wore braces for too long, too late in life.

When we enter the space I see that it's not much bigger than Juiceboxxx's room in Williamsburg, and is crowded with amplifiers and mixing boards and lord knows what else; a zebra print blanket covers one of the walls and the drum kit where Mike is sitting is on a raised platform resting on cinderblocks. It's really messy, with tangled up cords all over the floor and a row of special effects pedals that I'm guessing belong to Willy. "So are you guys just playing through the set?" I ask. Willy nods a little wearily as he tunes up his guitar, and Juiceboxxx, who is hunched over a laptop and looks to be queuing up some backing music, says, in a focused voice, "Yeah, man, we've just been doing it over and over since like five o'clock, trying to get it perfect."

I find a stool to sit on by the door and take out my notebook, hoping it doesn't make anyone too self-conscious, but after a few minutes of watching Juice and listening to the way he's talking to Willy and Mike about what he wants to accomplish with this next run-through of the set, it dawns on me that he is very much performing for me—that in his mind this is going to be a scene in whatever I end up writing, a glimpse into Juiceboxxx at work.

He takes off his jacket to reveal the same goofy HIGH ROLLER pot-leaf shirt he wore that first night we hung out in Max's brother's yard, and after making sure everybody's in position he gives a big nod to both Mike and Willy, who lock eyes for one second and then start the song. As Juice waits for his cue to come in, I take a breath as I realize something that has weirdly not occurred to me until this very moment, which is that I'm about to see Juiceboxxx perform live for the first time in what has to be at least five years.

I realize right away, just from the fact that Mike is staring at Juice the entire time he's playing, that what's happening here is that he is being trained, and that Willy and Juice could play these songs together in their sleep. The few times Juice stops the set to give notes, it's always to ask Mike to do something a little differently, or to make sure he remembers something he asked him to do earlier in the day. "Going into the part where everything drops out, do you wanna do a crash on the one?" he asks at a certain point, making me feel a sense of pride for being fairly confident that "a crash on the one" refers to hitting a particular cymbal on the first beat of every measure. "Just remember, no fills or anything—I feel like speed is really important on this one." Then he adds, with a smile, "I know drumming for me is boring as fuck." As he says these things I realize I'm seeing evidence of Juice's

surprising precision—the specificity of his vision, the delib-
erateness of the execution.

Not that it sounds all that great, I have to admit. As they
play through "Open Up Your Life" I can barely hear Juice's
vocals over Willy's guitar, and there's a general shaky loose-
ness to the whole thing that makes me worried, until I remind myself this band has been playing together for less than
two days. I can't tell how Juice feels about it, in part because
he's only going halfway through the motions, performing a
number of somewhat convincing rock-and-roll moves that
I gather he's ripping off from the likes of Springsteen and
Cheap Trick. As he leans forward with the mic stand in his
hands and shimmies with his hips, puts one hand behind his
back and bounces in place, does little kicks with his white
sneakers, throws his fists into the air, etc., I can tell he's trying to find some middle ground between actually practicing
and conserving his energy. Watching this makes me almost
regret that I didn't just wait to see the actual show.

"It's definitely getting there," Juice says after they finish "Never Surrender Forever."

"Is that what you're closing with?" I ask, and I'm thrilled when he says yes because it suggests he knows it's one of the best things in his repertoire.

When we go outside to take a break and get some air, I say, "So what'd you guys all do today?" which is always my go-to question whenever I find myself in a group where the dynamic is a little fragile and people don't totally know what to talk about. Juice says he actually had an exciting day— that he met with an important music industry guy named Dante Ross for almost three hours and got some really useful notes from him after playing him a bunch of his songs. I wonder if I should pretend to know who Dante Ross is but decide to just ask; it turns out he's an old-school artist development guy whose biggest claim to fame was launching the solo career of Busta Rhymes and getting the guy from House of Pain a record deal after he rebranded himself as a blues singer named Everlast. More recently, Juice says, he managed an extremely popular up-and-coming white rapper from Queens named Action Bronson. When I hear that it makes me think this guy could actually do something good for Juice if things go right.

I ask how the meeting came to be, and the answer is that Ross had just hit him up on Twitter. But when I ask if that's as promising as it sounds, Juice kind of waves it off, saying he's talked to big industry people before and it hasn't led anywhere. I gather he's referring to the six month period after he finished *I Don't Wanna Go into the Darkness* when he was in talks with Kanye West's manager and a couple of other label people that ultimately went nowhere. This was something Willy told me about over IM back when it was happening; it contributed, I gather, to Juice's sense that the album, which he ended up putting out himself, was under-appreciated and misunderstood.

After they play through the set a second time, Juice tells us about a party he went to in the Catskills a few nights earlier, hosted by some former record store owners who got priced out of Williamsburg and now spend their days and nights upstate throwing epic raves. It was a Halloween party, Juice says, so he wore a jester cap and brought devil sticks. This gives me a chance to tell a story I think will play well with this crowd, about how one summer at camp— not the one Willy and I went to but a different one—I performed a devil sticks routine in a talent show along to "Smells Like Teen Spirit." The story does go over well, which helps to slightly melt my sense of being an outsider among them, and makes me feel like something closer to one of the guys.

Before I head home, the band runs through their set one last time, and while it's basically the same as it was on the first two go-rounds, it's unmistakably sounding better, and I notice Juice does a lot of it with his eyes closed. This makes me think he's feeling more confident about Mike's drumming, since it means he doesn't have to give him subtle cues the whole time. It also confirms something for me in a very concrete way that I only knew in the abstract before—that these songs Juiceboxxx is playing, even the ones that are rambunctious and rowdy party anthems, are as deeply personal to him as anything you'd expect to hear from, say, a singer-songwriter known for confessional lyrics and emotional complexity. Juice is known for neither, and obviously that's not wrong. But watching him from three feet away as he plays through the glorious "21 on the 101," I see a guy who has successfully turned the raw materials of his life into art that will prove timeless—if not for a million people, then at least for me, and for Willy, and for lots of others who love Juiceboxxx and would be devastated if he ever gave up.

As the amps go quiet, Juice says it's time to call it a night and asks Mike if he can crash on his couch so that they can watch a 1997 live set by Beck that he thinks will really inspire them. As Willy and I wait for the subway together—I'm going home, he's going to his older brother's house—we talk about our jobs and our domestic lives, and he says something about how he and a lot of the friends he used to play music with in Milwaukee are trying to figure out what to do next. Molly, the girl who sang in Doom Buggy, has apparently enrolled in business school.

4.

As I count down the days to the beginning of the Thunder Zone tour, and more importantly, the night of the Brooklyn show I've had marked on my calendar since the beginning of

October, I find my obsession with Juiceboxxx growing more acute, to the point where any time someone asks me what I've been up to—over drinks, at parties, during dinner—I can't help but launch into a too-long account of how I've spent the past month interviewing and thinking about this guy who has loomed over me since I was a kid in ways I can't quite explain. It gets to the point where Alice can't really stand to listen to me talk about him, and actively extricates herself if she hears me start in on it with someone.

The morning of the show I wake up from a dream in which Willy was reunited with his old band from high school, and I got to see them perform as part of an all-day underground music festival on the second floor of some ramshackle house. In the dream, there was a big crowd gathered, and though I didn't know anyone there, I assumed everyone else was a fan of the band from long ago, like me. As they played I sang along to the words and did the dance I learned from Willy at that first church show until suddenly a mosh pit broke out, and I got shoved, violently, to the floor. When I got back up, winded and distraught, a big sweaty fat guy gave me a mean smile and said, "Sorry, bro. Figured you were up for it." That was the end of the dream.

In real life I stand in the shower and turn over a question in my head that's been bugging me since the night before: Should I send an e-mail to all my friends and encourage them to come with me to the show, or not? I imagine it, first, in the abstract: me watching Juiceboxxx by myself versus me showing him to people who have never seen him before, and playing a role in filling up the room in a way that might make Juiceboxxx and Willy happy. The second one seems more fun until I start thinking about who I'd actually invite, and how I would explain why this was something they should see. How would I get past the radioactive words I would have to use—"white rapper" and "rap-rock," chief among them—to describe what Juiceboxxx even was?

I decide to go alone.

Before getting on the subway I duck into Wendy's to pick up a few Jr. Bacon Cheeseburgers for the road and, after receiving a text from Juice that says "ur on the list," I briefly consider asking if he and Willy want me to bring them any food before deciding they probably have it covered. As I sit on the train and eat my burgers as discreetly as I can, I listen to the entirety of *I Don't Wanna Go into the Darkness* and feel inspired by the circumstances to try as hard as I can to hear it as if for the first time. One song jumps out at me in particular that never has before: a laid back, summery one with a beat that recalls the opening lines of the riff from "My Girl":

Hanging out, chilling on my porch up front
Nothing to do so we let the beat bump
Snackin' on pizza, messin' around
Just killing some time in this wasted town
And things aren't looking up
Yo man, they're looking down
Try to get a job but there's nothing to be found
But it's not as bad as it seems
'Cuz you can still dream.

I won't apologize for these lyrics. I think they're fantastic, and the way Juice delivers them is fantastic. The end of the song, too, takes my breath away, as the whole happy thing grinds to a halt and suddenly all I hear are a few clipped, ethereal notes and someone's raspy voice saying, over and over again, as if to bring me back down to earth, "Why are you even alive?"

5.

By the time I arrive at the Passion Lounge, it has started raining hard, and I am soaked. But I can see right away that the venue is magnificent, with a stage built high above the dance floor and an upside-down V-shaped staircase leading up to it that I can instantly imagine Juice making great use of during his performance. It's dark and hazy and there are neon lights in every color shining down and moving around the room from every direction. As I'm pulling out my ID to show the bouncer, I spot Willy and Juice and get so excited that I forget to say I'm on the list and end up paying the ten-dollar cover.

I can tell right away that Juice is stressed out, and I watch him as he says hello to people, clearly making an effort to be as friendly as he can because he's grateful to everyone who has come out despite the crappy weather. "I'm so fucking glad we're not playing at some DIY space," Juice says, kind of to me and Willy, but kind of to no one in particular. "No disrespect to those places, man, but this is just a different vibe." After that, Willy and I lose him until around 11:15, when he comes over and says in a quiet voice that he's not feeling great about the turnout. "I'm a little worried, man," he says, looking around and noticing all the empty space on the dance floor.

After he scampers off again Willy smiles and says he's not concerned, and that he's learned long ago not to ride the emotional waves that Juice goes through before every show, because he's invariably a pessimistic wreck until he gets on stage and is almost always totally satisfied afterwards. Last night, Willy says, they played in New Haven for four people and Juice felt really good about it anyway.

This talk of turnout, along with the considerable number of tequilas I've had since my arrival and the general sense of excitement building as showtime nears, jolts something in me, and in a fit of regret I decide that I was wrong not to invite any of my friends to the show. I pull my phone out and try to think of who I know who lives nearby, who could get here in fifteen minutes, and more importantly, would be willing to. Finally I decide to call Max, after remembering all of a sudden the interest with which he watched the Juiceboxxx documentary with me, and tell him to get in his car and drive over right away. He tells me he's sick and he can't. I beg him, but he says no. When I give up and put my phone away I'm bummed out for about five seconds but then I stop caring.

6.

While we wait for things to get rolling, I ask Willy if he still thinks Juice is on the verge of quitting. His answer makes me smile widely: "Actually," he says, "based on how he's been during this tour so far, it kinds of seems like being in New York has re-energized him."

Elated, I look over at Juice with this great news in mind. I notice a waitress giving him the five minute warning as he glances around the room and asks her to let him wait another ten so that a few more people have time to show up. Willy takes this as a cue to go start getting ready, while I find a place to stand near the front of the room and glance at the crowd. There are pretty girls in front of me and to my left, including one tall blonde with a backwards hat who has been dancing really hard to the music being played by the DJ since the moment she walked in. I notice there are a lot of tall guys with glasses, like me, but I recognize no one except Jacob and Kareema, who has a big camera around her neck and looks to be scouting angles from which to shoot the performance. I wave to them and they wave back.

Finally the music from the DJ booth goes quiet and is replaced by the beating of drums and the monster riff that Willy plays to open "Like a Renegade," one of Juice's biggest hits in terms of YouTube views. And with that, we're off, and when I take one last look around before things really get going, I see that the dance floor is, if not packed, then adequately crowded. There are people here who are extremely excited to see Juiceboxxx play, and as the beat pounds, they seem to be awaiting his arrival on stage with as much antic-ipation as I am. As the suspense builds I can't help but start bouncing on the soles of my feet and nodding my head to the beat.

Then Juice comes out, a cordless mic in hand, and starts stalking around the stage and practically skipping as he finds his rhythm. He looks huge up there on the balcony twenty feet above us, and as he moves from one side of the room to the other, the corners of his unzipped denim jacket flapping and his pale skin glowing through his white sleeve-less undershirt, I can't help but take note of the fact that he looks better than I've ever seen him, physically—lean, tall, broad-shouldered, his hair fashionably short. At some point he takes his jacket off, and when he raises his arms up, I can see the hair under his arms—something he has obviously had for years, but which strikes me in the moment as evi-dence that he has grown into something, that he is not some lost boy anymore but a man in control of his destiny. This is what I'm thinking about as he raps his first verse, delivering it with clarity and focus, and punctuating every line with a triumphant fist pump:

> *I had to get out of my town for a bit when it all went*
> *   down, yo, I couldn't quite face it!*
> *I dropped out and went on the road*
> *Nowhere to run, I got nowhere to go*
> *But now I'm at the show, and I'm playing, and I'm*
> *   slaying it*

Tomorrow I just don't know where I'm fuckin' staying at
And I know the choices that I have made . . .
LIVING LIKE A RENEGADE!

I'm singing along to every word and so are a bunch of people in my immediate vicinity. But it's when Willy and Mike start in on "21 on the 101" that the place really comes alive and Juice makes his way into the crowd. As he launches himself down the middle of the room I worry for a second that he's about to start crashing into everybody like he used to in the old days—basically, acting like he's in a noise band again—but instead he comes to a standstill, strikes a pose with his hips out and his arm way, way up, and I realize this is a very different Juiceboxxx than the one I remember.

Everything about his body language exudes control and confidence—from the way he's holding his mic stand as he leans over the lip of the banister, to the fearlessness of his exuberant scissor kicks, to the way he puts his arm around Willy and puts his head next to his so that they can sing the final part of "Open Up Your Life" together. At one point he leaps up onto an amplifier, his shirt off and his jacket back on, and he's shaking his hips and pounding the air with his fist. He looks like a total pro. More than once he runs back out into the crowd, which parts for him as if he's been shot from a bow and arrow. He's on his knees, then he's in the air, then he's standing with his legs spread three feet apart and his right hand behind his back.

About three quarters into the set he crouches down in the middle of the dance floor, looks up at Willy and Mike, and makes some kind of signal with his right hand.

Almost immediately the beat evens out and Willy starts palm-muting, as Juice launches into what I can tell right away is going to be an impassioned speech. "All right," he says, perched on one knee as the music continues to simmer behind him. "What we're gonna do right now is we're gonna go to that place called the next level. How many of you motherfuckers know about that?" Everybody, including me, screams and roars in approval. "That next level," he repeats, talking a mile a minute. "That's what your fuckin' parents warned you about. That's what your teachers warned you about. That's what your local city alderman warned you about! They said, 'Hey man, don't go to that next level, 'cuz if you go to that next level, you're gonna never come back!'"

With that he gets up on both feet and there is more screaming, more roaring, as he turns to face the crowd. "Well, I'm here to tell you, folks, that tonight, and only tonight, at the Passion Lounge in Brooklyn, New York, not only are we gonna go to the next level, we're gonna go to the level above the next level." He's sounding more and more like a carnival barker with every word and the room feels like it's hanging on for dear life. Finally, after a beat, Juice says, "That's right, ladies and gentlemen," and hits the punch line: "We're going to the NEXT NEXT LEVEL! Who's with me?"

As the crowd explodes into yelling and clapping, Juice mounts one of the speakers and stands up straight. He is now towering above us as he finishes out the song; moments later I hear the opening notes of "Never Surrender Forever," and Juice rejoins his bandmates on the balcony. The next four minutes are beautiful: Willy bangs his head as he plays guitar, Juice cradles the mic in his hands and wraps the Thunder Zone banner around his neck like a flag, Kareema stands on the stairs with a huge smile on her face and takes pictures. When Juice wanders out into the crowd during the guitar solo people tousle his hair and jump up and down like they're at a pop punk show. Everybody's singing, "Never surrender forever / Never surrender forever / Never surrender forever." As the last chord rings out Juice has his fist in the air and a big grin across his face.

7.

"That felt good," says Willy after the set. Juiceboxxx seems happy too, and I tell him how awesome I thought he was. When I go over to the merch table to have a look around, I find a cassingle of his that I never knew existed and a Juiceboxxx T-shirt that I've long wanted to own. Juice refuses to take more than ten dollars for both items, and insists on throwing in a free copy of the twelve-inch of "Sweat," even though I already own it, and an Extreme Animals CD even though he knows I'll probably never listen to it. When I tell him and Willy I need to go home Juice clasps my hand and brings me in for a quick hug.

On the subway ride back to my apartment I think about how much I love being his number one fan.

8

DREAM ON

1.

The next time Juice and I talk, it's on the phone. The tour is drawing to a close, and he sounds dead tired on the other end of the line, as well as slightly on edge because he knows Willy and Mike are waiting for him in order to start driving to Philadelphia. After the Passion Lounge show, Juice tells me, they drove to Chicago for the Midwestern leg of the tour, and have since come back east. Inconveniently, he says, he has developed a mild rash all over his body.

"That sounds terrible," I say, and after a bit of internal back and forth, decide to confess to him that on a semi-regular basis I get hives all over my torso, face, neck, and back. And so we talk about that for a while. "Mine just look like random red shapes, and as far as I've been able to figure they don't come on for any particular reason," I tell him, when he asks.

"Yeah . . ." he says in response, speaking slowly, clearly unsure where to go next with this and sounding a little shy and distracted. "I dunno, man. I dunno what the fuck this is. I don't think it's hives. But this whole tour has been relatively grueling—I mean, not super-grueling compared to some things I've done in the past, but you know. I feel like I'm pushing myself on this one more."

I ask him if part of the problem might be that he's out of practice, having been off the road for as long as he has, or that he's in charge of everything, and is responsible for taking care of logistics in a way that he didn't have to back when it was just him traveling alone with an iPod opening for random local bands.

"Yeah, maybe," Juice says. "Or maybe it's just because of going to New York, I'm kind of pushing myself toward something in general, because I'm just having clearer and clearer ideas of what I want to do with myself. And the clearer that gets the more clearly I see the amount of work I'm gonna have to do in order to achieve it."

I hate when he gets vague like this—it's by far my least favorite part of hanging out with him—so I ask him what he's imagining in particular. He talks around it for a full minute before I realize he's picking up the thread of our conversation from Grand Morelos, about his long-standing ties to various niche communities within underground music, which, if he had been smart, he would have distanced himself from by now. As he's talking I can tell he's nervous about sounding ungrateful, or coming off like he thinks he's better than all his friends who are still happily playing basement shows for each other, and going on tour in order to catch up with old acquaintances. But Juice clearly wants more, and as he continues to describe the moves he wants to make, his ambition starts to sound more and more real to me.

"I need to do something I haven't done yet," he says, "which is to make a truly transcendent record, you know? I think the live show is getting very close to where I want it to be in terms of something that can be put on the road, and can be put in front of, like, less counter-cultural audiences. But right now the only way for me to transcend certain communities I've been a part of since I was fifteen is just, you know, to make better music."

It is so cool to hear him say this, but I sense frustration behind the sentiment, because aside for the Passion Lounge show and maybe a few others, the Thunder Zone tour has taken place in exactly the kinds of DIY spaces that he's trying to get beyond. "I don't know if this is how the audience has been feeling but to me it just feels so clear that the show I'm doing now is not for these rooms anymore," he says.

He sounds exhausted but impatient, I think to myself—not to get off the phone with me, though maybe that too, but for the tour to end and for the rash to go away so he can start what has crystallized in his mind as the next phase of his life.

2.

The tour's been over for about a week when we meet up for what we've agreed will be our last interview. I ask him to come to my neighborhood again, to a diner called Clark's in the heart of Brooklyn Heights.

On my walk over I bump into my friend and sort-of neighbor Nate, who was a year above me in college and has recently become a staff writer at a big magazine. He is a soft-spoken guy who brings a delicate sensibility to all his stories; as a reporter his main strength isn't finding out secret facts or even spotting telling details the way you're taught to in journalism school, but in feeling and rendering with precision and sensitivity the mood of whatever or whoever he's writing about. I don't know how he does it, but when you read his pieces you're left with a sense that you have experienced the same gusts of emotion, the same hidden notes of pathos, that he did while working on it.

Nate has recently published a piece about Silicon Valley, and the young, entrepreneurial "creatives"—my word, not Nate's—who live there and collaborate on art projects with the backing of venture capitalists. The article freaked me out when I read it because it revealed to me yet another way I could have chosen to live my life but didn't, introducing me to these people in their early twenties who seemed to have created their own lanes in culture and achieved perfect freedom in the process. It reminded me, as so many things have been lately, that at twenty-eight years old, it's distinctly possible that I am who I am, and that it's too late to do anything about it.

Certain that Nate must have felt the same way when he was hanging out with these people, I had e-mailed him after reading his story and told him that, after a brief moment of envy, I ultimately did not find the zippy, well-financed scenesters he had written about inspiring. As free as they were and as much idiosyncratic fun as they seemed to be having, their existence seemed devoted more or less entirely to the optimization of their lifestyles, and therefore had a weightlessness to it that I did not associate with people—artists—who used their freedom and creativity to admirable ends.

In his response to me, Nate described a debate he had been having with his mother, about, as he put it, "the purpose of life." In her mind, he said, it was to collect experiences and memories, which was somewhat consistent with the way these Silicon Valley kids approached things. Nate, on the other hand, wanted to take all of his experiences and make of them something lasting—something that would outlive him, that would matter to people, and would scratch itself into the souls of strangers.

In my original e-mail to Nate I didn't mention that I had someone in mind I was comparing the Silicon Valley people to, but now that we're face to face and I happen to be going to meet that very someone for dinner, it kind of just tumbles out of my mouth. "I'm actually about to go interview a guy who sort of colored my reaction to your story," I say. When Nate invites me to elaborate, I find, as usual, that I don't have an effective summary at the ready of who Juiceboxxx is or why I'm so invested in him.

"He's a white rapper from Milwaukee who I met when I was sixteen," is how I start, but then interrupt myself because I realize, as I have over and over again during the past month, that it sounds unspeakably lame. Seeing me flail, Nate generously rescues me, and tells me I don't have to worry about explaining it on the fly. "But he sounds like a real character," he says by way of closing. I'm a little embarrassed as we say goodbye, but as I cross the street and turn the interaction over in my head I'm happy to realize that the run-in has clarified something for me. What I want to understand most desperately about Juiceboxxx is how he thinks about the purpose of his life.

As I make my way to Clark's, I wonder if it's the kind of thing I could just ask him straight out, even though I would normally think it ridiculous and inhumane to make someone formulate an answer to such a question on the spot. On the other hand, Juiceboxxx's entire body of work, all the way back to that first EP he put out as a freshman in high school, has explicitly been about dreams—about how all of us are always supposed to follow them, and how he, in particular, is never going to give up on his no matter how dark things get. It's a fair question, I think, to ask what those dreams he's always talking about actually consist of.

I realize I have no idea what he would say. Is it that he wants to be famous? Reviewed on *Pitchfork*? Taken seriously as a rapper in the same way other weirdo hip-hop outsiders like Lil B' and Riff Raff are? Though he's making art, it doesn't feel right to say that he's driven by anything like Nate's desire to leave behind a body of work, or even to "touch" people with his music. At the same time, I don't think he's like Nate's mom either, and he's certainly not like those people in Silicon Valley. I promise myself that I will figure this out tonight.

3.

When we sit down he asks me what I'm doing for the holidays, and I tell him I'm going to California to visit Alice's parents, then staying out there for a week of vacation during which I plan to go over all the notes I've taken on him since he arrived in October. I ask him whether he's going home for Christmas and he says he is, but that he's spending Thanksgiving in Philadelphia with his ex-girlfriend Frankie, who is in her late thirties now and married. Juice says he hopes to be back in New York in January, though nothing is set in stone, and everything depends on whether he has enough money to actually start a life here, and can find an apartment that is cheap enough for him to afford. There's that house in Far Rockaway, he says, where a bunch of his friends from the noise scene all live together for next to nothing, and if there's room for him there it would be totally ideal. But he can't exactly count on it.

When the waiter comes Juice orders a Caesar salad and I get a pork chop. Then, out of nowhere, Juice starts telling me about an artist he's really excited about—an experimental rapper named B L A C K I E who, according to Juice, has been extremely influential, but hasn't received credit for any of the breakthroughs he has catalyzed in American culture. This guy is always one step ahead, Juice says. He's an outsider who makes confusing music that puts him very much in his own universe.

I ask Juice if that's how he feels about himself, and he says, forcefully, no. "I feel like I'm much more calculated than someone like B L A C K I E."

After processing this for a moment—though I no longer think of Juiceboxxx as a pure "genius," Juiceboxxx as critic still doesn't totally compute—I sort of blurt out that I want him to talk to me about the future, and what exactly he'd like to see happen to his career from here on out. Though I instantly regret coming at him so abruptly, I'm relieved to see that he doesn't really seem to mind. By way of an answer he tells me a story about a tour he went on in Australia a few years back, during which he opened up for Big Freedia, a drag queen from New Orleans who has long enjoyed the status of a local legend, and can whip rooms all over her city into a frenzy.

"Having to open for her every night, I felt like I was touring with Little Richard or something, truthfully," Juice says. "Just seeing her completely devastate these Australian rooms for the first time ever and people just fucking climbing on the walls or whatever, just flipping out . . ."

The high point of the tour, he says, was getting to play

a festival in front of fifteen thousand people—the biggest crowd he had ever played for by a factor of at least ten, and a world away from the DIY spaces, dive bars, and basements in which he had done almost all of his performing up to that point. The set didn't go that well, he says, and there were scattered boos at the end, while he and Willy played the two minutes of feedback and abrasive white noise that they'd been closing all their shows with at that time. But even before that, Juice says, he felt like he just couldn't get the crowd's attention by doing what he normally did. And as painful as it was during the twenty minutes he was up there, it made him realize that if he wanted to get to that next next level, and really reach people on a large scale, he would have to learn to be a whole new Juiceboxxx.

As he's saying this I think to myself about "Open Up Your Life" and "Never Surrender Forever," and try to imagine seeing them performed in front of festival crowds, with huge throngs of people singing along, raising their fists, and putting their arms around their friends. I'm reminded of something Willy once said to me, about how in Juice's mind there are thousands of teenagers out there in America, all just waiting to be reached by someone like him.

"So, I mean, do you want to be a star?" I ask after a moment. "Do you think that would be fun?"

Juice smiles uncomfortably, shrugs, and says, "I don't know," then leaves it hanging there for a few seconds.

"I think you could be a star," I say, injecting my voice with a deliberate dose of boyishness in order to compensate for what might otherwise sound cynical or disingenuous. "I always thought that."

Juice looks around and takes a sip of his coffee. "Let me reframe this question," he says finally. "It's not really about fun for me. I'm not a weekend warrior. I'm not working a day job and playing basement shows on nights off or whatever. Music isn't my fucking kickball team, you know?"

I tell him I didn't mean to imply that it was, a little hurt that he'd think that was something he really needed to tell me at this point.

4.

After our food comes, Juice asks me if I've ever seen the show Kitchen Impossible. It's a reality show, he says, in which people who own failing restaurants are visited by consultants who help them rebrand their establishments by telling them what to change on the menu and how to redecorate. Usually, the restaurant owners don't want to take the advice, because they're so stuck in their ways and don't realize it's for their own good.

If there was a Rapper Impossible and he was on it, Juice says, the same thing would happen to him—and has, in fact, in the sense that every time some friend or fellow musician has told him to change his name, ditch all his baggage, and start over fresh, he has resisted even though he knows they're right.

"There are just so many flaws, just on a very practical

level, with what I'm doing," he says. "I think about it all
the time."

"Do you still think about quitting?" I ask, confident the
answer's going to be yes but hoping it'll be no.

"Truthfully?" he says, "I don't know what would happen
if I stopped doing this, or if I started, like, calling myself
by my real name. People are always telling me, like, 'Oh,
you could do other stuff.' And maybe I could. And maybe
five years from now I'll look back and be like, 'I can't believe I held onto this shit as long as I did.' But I don't know.
It's just been the most important thing in my life for so
long, man. And sometimes that bums me out, because I'm
just aware that maybe nothing will ever fucking happen,
and that maybe I'm just wasting my time and prolonging
the inevitable."

As I listen to him say this, I realize I have no idea whether
the end of the thought process is going to be optimism or
despair, so unpredictable are the leaps he tends to make
from one extreme to the other without any apparent provo-
cation outside of his own mind.

In search of clarity, I ask him what determines how he
feels about the future of Juiceboxxx at any given moment.
He responds by invoking the "Thunder Zone," that thing
he named his label after and is always talking about in his
songs. What it refers to, he explains, is the experience of
being trapped in between his relentless mood swings—the
experience of facing pure darkness, but trying to push it
back with all the thunder he can muster.

"It's like, destruction and redemption," he says. "This never-ending cycle of fucking up your life and hating yourself and then trying to move on and trying to keep doing what you love. Figuring out how to live with yourself despite who you are, or despite the decisions you've made. Despite failure."

Leaving Clark's Diner, we see that it has started raining, and after initially trying to explain to Juice how to get to the train he needs to take in order to get home, I decide to just show it to him, and so we run side by side down the street, holding sections of *The New York Times* that I had in my coat pocket above our heads as protection. When we reach the subway entrance, I quickly thank him for spending so much time with me while he was in town, and he thanks me for dinner. "Let's link up whenever I'm back, go to a party or something," he calls out to me, just before ducking underground. I yell back that that sounds good, and as we wave goodbye I realize I might not see Juiceboxxx again for a very long time.

POSTSCRIPT

1.

He ended up coming back, of course. And when he did, to my surprise, we started hanging out pretty regularly. One night he came over to my friend David's house and we watched Drake host *Saturday Night Live*—me, Juice, and like ten other people. Afterwards he and I sat around with my other friend Joe and his girlfriend Carrie, and the four of us talked happily about rap and listened to country songs that Juice played for us off his phone. At one point he told us about how he'd recently started writing and recording demos for a guy who managed country bands and had co-written a bunch of the songs on Taylor Swift's first record. After we parted ways he texted me, "thanks for the fun night."

There were more nights after that. One time we went to a dance club together. Another time I ran into him at a bar in Williamsburg. On one of the coldest nights of the winter, he invited me to a party at that house in the Far Rockaways where he had decided to live, after all. When I was getting ready to leave the party, at around four a.m., Juice pointed me in the direction I was supposed to go in order to get home, but told me that if I didn't feel like I could make the journey, I was welcome to just crash with him.

2.

In the spring, Juiceboxxx made the first live television appearance of his career, in connection with a musical festival taking place in Milwaukee for which he had traveled home. The local news brought him in for an interview about the event, to talk a little bit about his career as a rapper, and have him play one of his songs live in the studio.

The segment did not go well. During the Q&A portion, Juice looked dazed, and the skin around his eyes was disconcertingly dark, like he hadn't slept in days. Tall, lanky, dressed in all black, he swayed languidly back and forth, smiled a lot, and chattered in an unintelligible, rambling cadence about what it was like spending his life on the road. The two newscasters, a middle-aged man and woman, weren't sure how to react to him. "We love your energy!" one of them said.

Things got worse as soon as he started his performance. First his earpiece fell out, which meant he couldn't hear the backing track he was supposed to be rapping over. Then, when he got it back in, it became clear that the music was playing so softly in the studio that it was basically inaudible, both to him and to the people watching at home. All that came through was Juice's shaking voice and his panicked breathing disguised as laughter as he tried to get through his lines. The producers ended up cutting him off after about thirty seconds and went to commercial.

I only saw the video later, when Juice informed me by e-mail that it had "gone viral," popping up on a number of big sites, including *The Huffington Post*, as an irresistibly horrifying glimpse at an on-camera train wreck. "Wisconsin, you owe the world a very serious, heartfelt apology," one blogger wrote, in a post that declared Juiceboxxx to be the worst rapper of all time. "It's so fucking bad, we can't stop laughing at it," wrote another. Before long the clip made its way onto a late-night talk show, giving Juiceboxxx more exposure in under a minute than he'd had since he became who he was more than a decade ago.

As a result of all this attention, a bunch of people in Milwaukee started saying terrible things about Juiceboxxx—about how he didn't represent the city and had besmirched the local hip-hop community's name. But an elder statesman of the local scene named Doormouse, who ran that record store Juiceboxxx liked going to as a kid, wrote a long Facebook post defending his honor, as did DJ Kid Cut Up, a Milwaukee fixture who helped Juice with his first EP when he was still in high school.

A few weeks after things died down, Juice addressed the video on his blog. "I have never been a part of what you might call a 'viral shit-storm' but I guess that's what happened to me after this performance," he wrote. "I got a lot of hate/love and felt some pretty intense feelings coming my way. I don't really want to dwell on this minor blip in my insanely long, weird life of music but it is noteworthy."

Then, to close: "Ego annihilation isn't a bad thing and I've come out of this experience more excited about making and performing music than ever."

The next thing I knew, he was working on a new album, and in April he announced that he was going on tour again. This time the show would be called "Business As Usual." It would start at the beginning of May and last just under a month.

3.

It was about one week into the year 2015 that Juiceboxxx and I met up after we both got off work and I was forced to ask him that question about whether I had ruined his life. This was a few months after he started the job at my friends' art magazine, and I feared that the small but steady paycheck Juice was now drawing, thanks in part to my involvement in his life, had caused him to stray from the path that had always defined him. The most concrete manifestation of this, as I mentioned before, was that he was publishing articles under his own name, and also renting his own room in an actually decent apartment—one that he shared, coincidentally, with the keyboard player from Real Estate.

Even as I reminded myself that Juice had asked *me* about job leads, I hated myself for having played a role in making him more similar to me. I hated it, and I wanted desperately for him to tell me I was wrong to be concerned.

When I asked the question he smiled and, after a moment, lifted his index finger to his forehead. "You see this?" he said, pointing out a large, violet wound that I had been assuming was the leftover trace of a scratched off pimple. It turned out it was the result of Juice hitting himself in the head repeatedly with a microphone, while performing at a New Year's Eve party in Chicago about a week earlier.

"Things got really unhinged," he said. "I was bleeding everywhere, and usually I don't draw blood when I do that. Somehow I felt like I had to prove something to myself, I guess."

Is it weird, I asked him, to have some semblance of stability for the first time in his life?

"No," he said, waving me away. "It's great. And I don't feel that stable, by the way—you should see my room."

I smiled at this but didn't say anything, and Juice continued talking.

"I mean, what else would I be doing right now?" he said. "Still living in that basement in Far Rock? This is better. This isn't ideal, but it's better."

I told him, with some hesitation, about the thing Willy had said to me more than a year earlier, about how if Juiceboxxx got a proper job and put down roots on the East

Coast, it could mean the end of the Juiceboxxx project as we all knew it.

Juice laughed at this and broke eye contact.

"No," he said. "It's far from done, sadly. I'm still doing everything."